# HEALING IN THE HOLY LAND

**GLEN NATALIER**

Published in Australia by Sid Harta Publishers Pty Ltd,
ABN: 46 119 415 842
23 Stirling Crescent, Glen Waverley, Victoria 3150 Australia
Telephone: +61 3 9560 9920, Facsimile: +61 3 9545 1742
E-mail: author@sidharta.com.au

First published in Australia 2019
Copyright © Glen Natalier 2019
Photographs © Glen Natalier 2019
Cover design, typesetting: WorkingType (www.workingtype.com.au)

The right of Glen Natalier to be identified as the Author of the Work has been asserted in accordance with the Copyright, Designs and Patents Act 1988.

The Author of this book accepts all responsibility for the contents and absolves any other person or persons involved in its production from any responsibility or liability where the contents are concerned.

All rights reserved. No part of this publication may be reproduced, stored in a retrieval system, or transmitted, in any form or by any means without the prior written permission of the publisher, nor be otherwise circulated in any form of binding or cover other than that in which it is published and without a similar condition being imposed on the subsequent purchaser.

Natalier, Glen
*Healing in the Holy Land*
ISBN: 978-1-925230-55-0
pp228

## About the Author

Glen Natalier was born into a closely-knit rural community in the Lockyer Valley in Queensland, Australia. He chose not to stay on the family farm but completed the necessary studies to become a high school teacher of geography and German language. During these teaching years, he wrote several geography text books directed towards the syllabus requirements at that time. This allowed him to travel widely,  collecting, first hand, material and photographs which he used in these books. Years of teaching have left him with a love of learning and he finds that writing helps detract from the cares and worries which always seem to arise.

The tennis balls and footballs of previous years have morphed into golf balls which bring him great pleasure when seen against the green of the centre of a fairway.

Now retired, he lives with his wife, Jill, in a town just over a few hills from where he was born. Their four children and their families are scattered around Australia.

Glen's first novel *Sunrise in the West* was published in 2017.

The Jerusalem Cross was originally used as an emblem of the Kingdom of Jerusalem during the Crusader era. It now indicates those pilgrim sites under the Franciscan Custody of the Holy Land.

*To my wife, Jill.*
*Whose love and encouragement*
*Never waivered.*

*Looking across to old Jerusalem from the Mount of Olives. The Dome of the Rock, an important Islamic shrine, stands on the Temple Mount where the second Jewish temple was previously situated.*

# Acknowledgements

Two years ago I was fortunate enough to be a member of a tour party visiting Israel. The tour advertising brochure billed the trip as a **Pilgrimage to the Holy Land**. Naturally it concentrated on visiting those sites which have special reference and importance to the Christian religion.

This book grew out of that tour but is not a personal memoire of it. The sites mentioned are clearly actually places which feature on most tour itineraries, but the characters depicted are not based on tour members. They are my creations in attempting to introduce description and discussion around many of the pilgrimage sites which were visited.

I do however feel it necessary to thank the Tour Leader, Graeme Lienert, and the official Israeli Guide, Gale Mashiach, whose knowledge and professionalism made for a memorable trip. Many thanks also to my travelling companions who helped make the whole experience so enjoyable that I was moved to write this book.

I wish also to thank my wife, Jill, who encouraged me to go on this pilgrimage. Little did she realise then that it would lead to many hours with me sitting alone in front of our computer while she read in another room.

Thanks also to Sid Harta Publishers and the team there, especially Barbara and Luke, who took on the job of turning my often-disjointed writing into this handsome volume.

God bless us all.

*An ancient olive tree in the Garden of Gethsemane.*

# Contents

| | | |
|---|---|---|
| Prologue | | 1 |
| 1 | Welcome to Israel | 7 |
| 2 | The Mount of Olives | 15 |
| 3 | Triumphant Entry | 25 |
| 4 | Shepherds' Field | 33 |
| 5 | Bethlehem | 41 |
| 6 | Jerome | 49 |
| 7 | First Night Dinner | 57 |
| 8 | Reprise | 65 |
| 9 | Hezekiah's Tunnel | 69 |
| 10 | Masada | 79 |
| 11 | Dead Sea | 87 |
| 12 | Remembering Easter | 97 |
| 13 | Sunday Worship | 105 |
| 14 | Jericho | 111 |
| 15 | Temptation | 117 |
| 16 | On the Sea of Galilee | 125 |
| 17 | Ancient Galilee Boat | 131 |
| 18 | Beatitudes | 143 |
| 19 | Simon Peter | 151 |
| 20 | Yom Kippur | 163 |
| 21 | In the Synagogue | 171 |
| 22 | Cana | 177 |
| 23 | Into the West | 185 |
| 24 | Jaffa | 193 |
| 25 | Sarona | 209 |
| 26 | Shalom | 215 |

*Palm tree backed by rugged landscape of the Judean Desert.*

# Prologue

## In Adelaide:

The seminar room was abuzz with the comments and ideas relevant (some perhaps not so) to the topic set for discussion. Most members of each small group were enthusiastically engaged in their task. These were so keen that it was often difficult, even for the most agile mind, to keep account of what was being aired. Others were less enthused, and their occasional comments were delivered mainly as a side-track. This could annoy the leader for the session as he was responsible for presenting a summary of his group's deliberations to the whole class the next day. The subtle peer pressure and lecturer expectation was high, and he felt obliged to be conscientious in carrying out his duty. He would try his utmost to be aware of all the comments flying about, would always be keen to keep the discussion moving and more importantly, keep the comments on topic.

Today's specific topic concerning Jesus' Sermon on the Mount had not fully engaged everyone. There had been many unhelpful comments.

'Well, what have we got so far?' One group's leader was endeavouring to organise the scattered ideas which had already been put forward and had shown some relevance.

'Nothing much,' was the candid assessment coming from one member.

But the leader was taking his job seriously. 'But there must be some reason why Matthew talks about the Sermon on the Mount, whereas Luke says that it was given on the flat land.' This was an attempt to bring the group back on task and to come to grips with the topic which had been set. 'Here, I'll read what my King James Version says in Luke: *And he came down with them and stood in the plain.*'

At this point he was interrupted by an obvious question: 'Can we be sure both Matthew and Luke are talking about the same episode?' Everyone looked around waiting for a response, but there was no opinion forthcoming.

'You would have to agree that everyone these days calls it the Sermon on the Mount. Surely that must tell us something,' contributed the fourth member of the group. 'Matthew calls it a mount, so either the sermon was definitely delivered up on a hill somewhere or Luke had a good reason for shifting Jesus down onto the plain. Let's just go along with what Matthew says and get on with the real discussion.'

But the leader persisted. 'I know he says mount, but as I have just read, Luke says a plain. No way can you say that a mountain is a plain.'

'Could we call it the Sermon on the Plateau?'

All eyes turned to the source of this suggestion but chose to ignore it.

'Oh, and another thing,' the same person continued. 'I've read somewhere that these beatitudes are merely a collection of what Jesus said as he was going around preaching, and so there was no "sermon" as such. On the basis of this, I suppose you could say that it was on both the mount and the plain, or on neither depending on how you define "sermon" here.'

'So, what is it that we are really discussing, or should be discussing? We seem to be getting nowhere,' the quiet, meditative member of the group made his contribution in an endeavour to avoid the confusion the previous speaker was causing.

The leader looked at the source of this question somewhat exasperatedly, but replied civilly, 'We are discussing whether

Matthew's version of the Sermon on the Mount is his attempt to show Jesus as the new Moses on a new Mt Sinai.'

'Oh, I see. Seems a reasonable suggestion to me. It also reads as though we should take the mount as a given, and not be arguing whether Jesus was on the plains, in the mountains or just wandering around.' The quiet, meditative thinker of the group had not contributed much to date. He would often create ripples in the lecture rooms with his flippant comments on topics which were considered more serious. No one could deny his knowledge of the Bible. It was his understanding and interpretation which often caused eyebrows to be raised. Before anyone could ask him to give his reasons for saying that he saw it as a reasonable suggestion he continued, 'And something just came to mind talking about all these mountains. Did any of you see the game between Mt Lofty and Port last Saturday? Or watch it? It was broadcast, I think.'

Four pairs of puzzled eyes turned in his direction, their heads all shaking. As no one gave a clear answer, the leader replied, 'It appears not. But I'll tell you what. I'll tack your question onto the end of my summary of our session today. That is, if I can get enough ideas to make a report. I've no doubt the Prof. will be able to say "yes" to your question, for he never misses a Port match.'

'No, on a serious note. I was really interested if any of you had seen the game and saw how Andrew played. I was there, and I've never seen him play so badly. He played without any energy and that's not like him at all. Besides that, he doesn't seem to have been at classes all this week. Well, he's not here now, is he? He is supposed to be in our group this month. I'm wondering if there is something wrong with him. Is he sick or something?'

\* \* \*

## In Melbourne at the same time:

Far from the academic halls and aisles of the Theological Academy in Adelaide, and with its eight-posted football grounds temporarily forgotten, Andrew Wagner was still being challenged. He was attending a Luther Conference commemorating 500 years since the German monk, Martin Luther, began a church reformation in Europe. Leading Luther scholars from around the world had been invited to present papers based on their individual Luther interests which would be relevant to the present times. Clergy, scholars and interested laypeople from many countries were in attendance.

As a teenager, Andrew had attended a Lutheran College in his home state of Queensland and this began his interest in the sixteenth century church reformer. That interest had continued to grow, so that after a few years he had left his engineering job at the local council and commenced studying to become a pastor in the Lutheran Church. At 25 years of age, healthy and fit and abounding in enthusiasm for his future career, he had forsaken the roads around Brisbane, left a small hole in the Western Magpies AFL team and headed to Adelaide to study theology.

His eighteen months there had been very productive and personally rewarding. He slotted seamlessly into the required courses at the Theological Academy, and the Mt Lofty Football Club obtained a talented mid-fielder. Above all he was a gifted and dedicated student always ready to help and advise anyone who was looking for help.

Now having taken the opportunity of attending a world class conference, focusing solely on Martin Luther, Andrew was ensuring that no session was missed. Meal and snack times were also of a high standard and he was enjoying these times as well. Apart from the culinary delights, these were times to meet people from many parts of the globe all of whom had an interest in Martin Luther and his theology. Strangers could approach one another knowing that the recent keynote paper would provide ample avenues for conversation.

It was morning tea time and an older man approached Andrew who had just selected a number of sweet, colourful tarts to go with his coffee.

'Hello, I'm Gordon,' he began by introducing himself. Then, looking carefully at Andrew's name tag, he continued, 'Andrew. I see that you are a theological student. Studies soon finished, are they?'

'I wish. This is only my second year down in Adelaide. No, in actual fact I don't really wish that the course was finished, for I enjoy studying.'

'Good for you! So, you are enjoying the conference? Hearing anything to challenge you?'

'Challenging! I think most people here would be finding something to challenge them. It's certainly a step above reading a few sections out of Luther's *Table Talk*. How have you been finding it?'

'Tough, to be honest,' replied Gordon. 'Luther's theology at this level is not my cup of tea.'

'You're not a pastor or academic, then?' Andrew posed the question.

'No, I retired early from the army and I now spend my time as a tour leader. I take groups to different destinations around the world, especially to Israel and Germany. I'm here mainly to get to know people and yes, let's be honest, to advertise a few of my trips that are coming up.'

'Lucky you,' Andrew had to say. 'I've never got round to travelling like a lot of other young people.'

'What!' replied Gordon. 'Never had any great desire to travel?'

'Probably it was a lack of finance rather than anything else,' was Andrew's honest reply.

'How would a trip to Israel, a pilgrimage to the Holy Land, strike you?'

'I've never really given it any thought. Even if I had the money I would find other ways of spending it. And now with my studies, I don't have the time to travel. And Israel? No, it wouldn't be very high on the list of places I would choose to visit.'

'I can understand that, but now that you are studying to be a minister of religion a trip there could open up a whole new world of understanding. Have you ever considered ...?' Here Gordon was interrupted by a bell calling everyone to the next session on the program. When the ringing had finished he continued, 'It seems we have been summoned. Anyway, great to have met you, Andrew. And oh, here. It's a brochure of my next Holy Land tour. Something for you to browse through if the next speaker doesn't hold your attention.'

Andrew took the brochure and shoved it into his folder of conference papers, train timetables, tissues and tourist maps. Then, in spite of feeling a little unwell from a slight headache and sore throat, he headed towards the lecture hall. Here he hoped the speaker would further his understanding of Luther's theology of giving and the gift.

# Chapter 1

# Welcome to Israel

The planes had landed. The travellers had emerged tired and dishevelled. The River Jordan had been crossed. This proved to be easier than in Joshua's day. Now with its passengers full of expectation the bus was travelling through the Promised Land to Jerusalem. Friends and strangers (mostly strangers), young and old (mostly old), were assembling for their pilgrimage. Finally, their waiting was over. For them, the journey was now beginning.

All were there for some reason. Whatever motivated them to join this Holy Land pilgrimage however, had been temporarily forgotten in the excitement of finally beginning their adventure. Those individual reasons, the motivating factors which had them eagerly signing on to the tour, would not remain suppressed indefinitely. They would no doubt resurface as Biblical sites were visited, as surprises emerged, as disappointments were experienced. They were the touchstones on which the trip would be continually assessed.

Would the reality of walking where Jesus may have trod fulfil everyone's expectations? A pilgrimage to the Holy Land may strengthen one's Christian faith; but then again it may not.

The adventure began by dining together. This getting-to-know-you, welcome dinner in a reserved section of the Dan Hotel's dining room in Jerusalem was at the coffee and yawning stage. For this group of Australian tourists, the twelve-day pilgrimage to the Holy Land had officially commenced. The tour leader, Gordon Lange, had said all the right things and the enthusiasm and expectation emanating from each member of the group was very evident. The official spiritual leader of this party, Pastor Paul Rider and his wife, Julie, had been introduced. A few wondered about the nature of his specific role but assumed that it would become clear as the tour progressed. The Israeli tour guide, Sarah, was welcomed with wild applause and the hint of a wolf-whistle from one of the back tables.

For most of those present, this occasion was the conclusion of many months of eager waiting and anticipation. This was a once-in-a-lifetime opportunity to follow in the footsteps of their Lord and strengthen their Christian faith. Andrew Wagner and his long-time friend Anthony (Tony to most) Jackson, however, had a mere three weeks to prepare for this unexpected journey to Israel. Now in Jerusalem, tired but contented, they, like all the others, were looking forward to what the next two weeks would bring.

It was only a month ago, while recuperating in Brisbane and waiting to see if the endless medical tests would point to some ongoing problem, that Andrew had been intrigued by an e-mail which arrived out of the blue. It was from Gordon Lange, an overseas tour leader, whom he had met briefly at a conference in Melbourne. Apparently sometime after that casual meeting over morning tea at the conference, Gordon had contacted Andrew's Theological Academy in Adelaide in an attempt to track him down. Gordon was anxious to contact Andrew to see if he would be interested in the upcoming trip to Israel, but the reluctance of the authorities at the Academy to give out any specific information had forced Gordon to use other methods to locate him. He eventually became aware of Andrew's on-going health problems and that he had taken a break from his studies. Feeling sympathy for this young man who had seemed so devoted to preparing for his future vocation, he had subsequently approached him with a generous offer.

Gordon explained that he knew of a benefactor who was willing to cover Andrew's costs if he wished to accept an invitation of going on the tour to Israel. 'After all,' Gordon had said, 'it's just what you need to take your mind off your illness. You would come back a new man. And in my mind, all theological students should have the opportunity of visiting the Holy Land.'

Andrew was finally convinced, but only after his friend Tony agreed to accompany him, to take good care of him and to bring him back home safely.

After the welcome dinner Andrew and Tony were in their hotel room wondering at the unusual chain of events which had got them there, but pleased nevertheless, and excited to be in Israel.

'Well, here we are!' said Andrew. 'Who would have thought?'

'Yes, it's crazy,' replied Tony. 'You have never really wanted to see Israel, and I never in my wildest dreams thought of coming here. Bali or Thailand, yes, but Israel? Yet here we are.'

'I wonder what we are in for in the next few weeks. I hope I can keep up with everything and everyone and not be any trouble.'

'Don't worry about that,' dismissed Tony. 'I'll look after you. But to tell you the truth I was a little disappointed when I saw all those who were in the group.'

' Disappointed? What do you mean?' Andrew asked.

'Come on, let's be honest. Was there anyone in the group that took your eye?'

'Heavens above,' said a rather shocked Andrew. 'This isn't *The Love Boat*.'

Tony laughed. 'But I'll tell you one thing. That tour guide isn't bad-looking. I'm sure I saw a twinkle in her eye when she looked at us during her introduction.'

Andrew shook his head. 'I don't think you should have wolf-whistled her when she was being introduced. And that twinkle in her eye you thought was there was probably more of a censure.

I thought it was a look of disapproval and that she was looking directly at me.'

'We'll see,' Tony was someone who seldom took 'no' for an answer. 'Anyway, I'm going for a good look around the hotel. I want to see what the bar is like and what else there is on offer. Coming?'

'No. I'm all done in,' replied Andrew. 'I'll sit out on the balcony for a while and relax before hitting the hay.'

Andrew was soon sitting comfortably watching the lights of suburban Jerusalem through the leaves of the date palms on the hotel's terrace. 'Well, I'm here,' he thought. 'The delayed plane, the long waits, the missed connections didn't make for a great trip. I suppose that's international travel these days. Then there was that young woman sitting opposite me at the airport who had each fingernail painted a different colour. I had then looked down to see if her toes had the same treatment. She must have misread my motive for she then pulled her short skirt closer to her knees, picked up her bags and moved off to a different seat.'

Andrew smiled to himself. Goodness knows what would have happened if Tony had been with him then. His eyes flickered a few times and then they shut. His head drooped.

*I hear my two-year-old nephew running around on the veranda. He shouldn't be here! He lives in Albury, not Brisbane. But who else could it be? Yes, it has to be him. It sounds as though he is fine-tuning his emerging language skills: 'Pane! Pane.' I hear him shouting. I pause, I listen, and I look up searching in front of the loud noise dropping from the clouds. I soon see the huge four-engine Airbus (or is it a Boeing Jumbo?) high to the south with a flying kangaroo attempting to catch up to the engines some metres ahead. Well, not so high really. At 20 kilometres out from the airport it still has much more climbing to do. It, however, has already begun its journey.*

*As it disappears into the distant haze I too let my imagination fly me with it to ... to where?*

*It is an escape to foreign climes. In the shrinking world of the twenty-first century are there foreign climes? Isn't this really a carry-over from Victorian times? What new is there to explore which hasn't been shown (with many repeats) on the Adventure Channel or National Geographic Channel? The world has been reduced to a 102cm flat plasma screen.*

*I have been allocated a window seat. Is this better than an aisle seat? Debates have raged, duels fought over this question. I personally remain quite neutral. Each seat can be as uncomfortable as any other. But today I have been lucky (or have I?) and have the advantage (or is it?) of a window seat. I look out of the window and what do I see? The plane's wing and its massive engines? No, I'm seated further to the front. The top of clouds? No, when they are not there hindering my view, what do I see? I see the page of an atlas. Watercourses meandering across the page and fading into the distance. Dots of settlement. Land patterns. The wrinkles of mountain ranges. All so remote, sketched, so detached from reality. Where are the personal struggles, the lovers' tiffs, the daily grind of existence?*

*Modern aeronautical technology lifts us above the mundane. From 10 000 metres there are no international borders, no power struggles. The trouble spots of the world pass unnoticed. The modern magic carpet has created a world of its own, a world apart. This world is especially woven to display its own reality. On it one appears to be very insecurely attached to the earth. Here is a world of its own. Qantas or*

*Emirates, Air China or China Airlines — it matters not at all. The feeling is the same, the experiences similar.*

*And then finally — it can seem like tiring eternity — with a change in revs, a decreasing speed and altitude the plane delivers me back to the real world with a slight bump, screeching tyres and roaring engines. Still strapped tightly to my out-of-this-world experience I arrive at the assigned gate. Only then am I released for my journey to continue. Buffeted by other people's overweight and oversized carry-on luggage I become part of a caterpillar emerging from a long tunnel to claim my luggage at the carousel. I wait. Round and round, the same cream case, the same bulging backpack. Should they be in Amsterdam perhaps, and not Amman? Is this where I really am? I wait. Why are my cases always the last to appear on the carousel? Does anyone's case come out first?*

*Finally through the suburbs to the hotel. Past dwellings crowned with defoliated forests tuned in to the local TV channels. Televisions, all made in China, attempting to standardise the world — a reversed Babel — but being strenuously resisted with a no, nein, nyet, siyo, lo. Wait a minute. Are they succeeding? Relaxed now in the hotel room, showered, shaved, rehumanised, I flick on the TV and CNN speaks to me in English, as it has always done. Does the hotel room TV set (made in China) default to CNN when switched on? Or does it merely have a personal disagreement with the antenna on the roof which is determined that it speak German, or Russian, or Swahili, or Hebrew?*

'Bei mir bistu shein. Please let me explain; Bei mir bistu ...'

Andrew was awakened by the powerful tenor voice of his travelling companion. It took him a few moments to realise he was on the balcony of their Jerusalem hotel and not flying to ... to where?

'Tony, what on earth is all that racket?'

'Just singing. Now that we are in Israel I though a few appropriate songs...'

'But what you are singing is Yiddish. They speak Hebrew here.'

'Well, how about a little dancing then?' asked an enthusiastic Tony, who began swaying, started a rhythmic kicking and then burst out, '*Hava nagila. Hava nagila, ve nismecha.*'

'For heaven's sake what have you been drinking, Man? We'll have the manager banging on our door soon.'

'OK, enough for tonight, but I hope we get the opportunity for some singing and dancing on the trip. I'm sure that good-looking guide knows a thing or two and could teach us a few fancy steps.'

'Keep your dreaming until you're in bed. I'm tired and I need to get a good night's sleep too. I must be even tireder than I had thought. You know, I've just had a most unusual sort of dream. I seemed to be talking to someone, but I don't know to whom. I was travelling to somewhere, but it wasn't really to here. Didn't know where I was headed.'

'*Fly me to the moon,*' Tony began singing again.

'For heaven sake, Tony, I don't need you to sing me a lullaby or whatever.'

*Dark olives growing on the Mount of Olives.*

## Chapter 2

# The Mount of Olives

The bus was being loaded and the passengers were looking around as they slowly stepped up through the door to see which seat might be most comfortable and best positioned. As soon as Leader Gordon determined the head count to be correct, Driver Masoud steered the coach out of the front driveway of the hillside Dan Hotel. The proper part of this Holy Land pilgrimage had begun for this Aussie group. Andrew and Tony, like two naughty school boys, had gone straight to the back seat and were now surveying their travelling companions.

'Say Andrew, look. Those two… one, two, three, four seats up… and the girl sitting opposite them. I don't remember them being at the welcome dinner last night. Do you?' Tony asked.

'No, I don't believe I do,' Andrew replied.

'I wonder if she belongs to them,' continued Tony.

'If she does, I'm sure they will be keeping a strict eye on her,' laughed Andrew. 'They probably have been told about you already.'

The short drive to the Mount of Olives lookout was made longer by the static rendition of *Jerusalem the Golden* over the PA system but happily shorter by the excited chatter of the passengers. Soon everyone had gathered in the lookout area, which being the party's first stop for the day, was not yet overcrowded.

Andrew stood looking across the Kidron Valley to Jerusalem. The sky was summer blue. The city was a broad sweep of dull dun with a scattering of dark and olive green. Central to all of this was the glittering golden dome set on its blue base. This beautiful building was the Dome of the Rock, one of Islam's holiest shrines. Many, like him, have stood at this point on the Mount of Olives and reflected on what they saw and what unfortunately they couldn't see. He looked around and witnessed people sobbing with emotion, overcome by what they saw and felt.

The Mount of Olives is a chain of low mountains running north/south to the east of Jerusalem, right on its doorstep. A good place for growing olives, one might assume from its name. The land descends from the lookout, crosses the narrow Kidron Valley and arrives at the eastern wall of the old city. The hills are some 800 metres above sea-level, and slightly above the height of Jerusalem. From the mount one can look across the steep-sided Kidron Valley and down onto the holy city.

Pastor Paul focused the thoughts of the group back 2000 odd years to the events which caused this small dot on the surface of the earth to become an important element in the history of Christianity.

It was spring in the year 36 CE (or 33 CE or 30 CE, for uncertainty surrounds the actual year when Jesus' final appearance in Jerusalem took place). The feast of the Passover was approaching, and thousands of pilgrims were making their way towards Jerusalem from the surrounding countryside as well as from other distant countries. Included in these numbers were no doubt many of Jesus' followers from Galilee. Some of these were worried and they were asking around if anyone knew whether Jesus also would be coming to the feast (John 11:56). Why were they concerned? The word was out that the Chief Priests and Pharisees had put a price on Jesus' head and were looking for co-operation from the public. Anyone knowing his whereabouts should let them know so that he might be arrested (John 11:57).

Jesus had previously indicated that he knew that he was

walking into a very dangerous situation but he was determined to continue his mission and so he made his way resolutely towards the holy city.

The biblical record notes that Jesus and his close disciples had been making their way south from Galilee. He had passed through Jericho and was now approaching Jerusalem from the east. Just ahead lay the Mount of Olives on which were a number of villages including Bethany and Bethphage. There was previous mention of Bethany in the Gospels but not of Bethphage. Bethany was located 3.5 kilometres east of Jerusalem. Today it is known as El-Azariah, a name which carries a tradition relating the area to Lazarus, who according to the story in John's Gospel (11:1-44),was the brother of Mary and Martha who lived in the village, two close friends of Jesus. Because of this relationship we can assume that Jesus stayed in their house during this visit to Jerusalem. It was a small rural village, probably with a population of around 200.

Bethphage appears to have been a similar type of village a little further along the road to Jerusalem. It is thought to have been situated at the present location of At-Tur, just before the crest of the Mount of Olives. These two villages — Bethany and Bethphage — as well as others scattered throughout the mountain area were located in farmland pockets which provided much of the fruit and vegetables for the city.

'Yes,' thought Andrew, 'many years ago Jesus also stood here, probably close to where I am now standing, saw the Holy City and reflected on what he saw.' *O Jerusalem, Jerusalem, you who kill the prophets and stone those sent to you, how often I have longed to gather your chickens together, as a hen gathers her chicks under her wing, but you were not willing. Look, your house is left to you desolate.*

This passage from Matthew's Gospel illustrates very clearly how Jesus thought about his ministry. He had spent the last few years trying to bring change to Jewish society, trying to establish, as he called it, the Kingdom of God; but the opposition had been too powerful. He felt he had not achieved the success he would have wished for.

What did Jesus actually see when he stood here those many centuries ago? The blue sky would not have altered. The dull, dun colour of the buildings, local limestone, would have been the same, although much less extensive than what is seen today. Andrew suspected that there would have been larger patches of dark and olive green. Central to his gaze also would have been the glittering gold, but the gold of a square and not a dome which visitors now see. The spectacular gold that Jesus saw was the gold of their holy temple; the earthly dwelling-place of their God. But he saw more than this.

Jesus looked. He looked through the cityscape spread out before him. He was sad and sombre as he reflected on the likely future of this city. Andrew also looked and saw more than the dull limestone buildings. He was saddened as he reflected on what the past 2000 years had done to this City of God.

Jesus looked and, like the prophets of old, saw the imminent destruction of a people whose hearts had wandered from the God of their ancestors. Here was once again the farmer prophet, Amos, who saw the religious leaders exploiting the poor. Here once again was Jeremiah warning Jerusalem of its approaching calamity. But Jesus' immediate future lay in this city. It lay here with the religious elite who spurned the general public. It lay here with the temple officials who cared mainly for themselves. It lay here with the High Priest and his advisors who collaborated with the enemy rulers. It lay here with the Roman soldiers patrolling the streets. It lay here waiting to claim the life of this Galilean prophet.

The Mount of Olives was a watershed in Jesus' life. He knew

what fate awaited him in that city across the Kidron and he could have turned back. He could have headed back down to Jericho, north along the Jordan river back to the relative safety of rural Galilee. He didn't. He chose to continue his life's calling to the end. His end would be on a hill just outside the walls on the other side of the city.

What exactly was in the thoughts of the people in the various tour groups which now began converging on this historic lookout point? Whatever it was one can assume that Jesus occupied a large part of most.

Andrew had moved to the railings of the lookout when he arrived. He leant there, thinking, meditating. So intense was his concentration on the scene in front of him that he was unaware that two ladies had moved up beside him. Margaret Schneider and Avril Baumgartner were long-time members of a Lutheran congregation in rural Victoria. They had been raised in devout Christian homes and most of what they had learnt in Sunday School and later in attending confirmation lessons had stayed with them. They could still proudly recite Bible texts which they had memorised sixty and more years ago. This visit to Israel was to be an emotional and highly religious experience for them.

Margaret's husband had died a few years previously and she was thankful that her friend, Avril, would accompany her on the trip. It was mooted initially that Avril's husband might come as well, but when he started saying that the farm could not get along without him and how he would feel like a rose between two thorns, only two tickets were purchased.

They were now thrilled to be standing where Jesus had been.

Margaret opened the conversation. 'Looking out there, can't you feel Jesus' presence?'

Andrew looked at them, two women visibly overcome by the emotion of the occasion. 'Honestly,' he replied, 'at the moment

I can't actually feel Jesus' presence. There are too many distractions for that. What I was thinking is how different it would have been here when Jesus was about.'

'Different in what way?' Avril wanted to know.

'Well, I was thinking particularly about the appearance of the place. Look at all the graves there. The whole hillside is a cemetery. And what about the vegetation that would have been here then?'

'Oh,' said Margaret, 'that hasn't really struck us, has it, Avril?'

The two women then looked at one another, puzzled, wondering how someone standing here on the Mount of Olives could see gravestones rather than Jesus, could feel saddened by the lack of vegetation and not feel the emotion of being here. Then Margaret continued, 'But let's go over there and see if we can get a better look at where Pastor Paul said the City of David was located.'

With this the two left Andrew looking across at thousands of years of human endeavour.

Others, however, were not content in just standing and looking but were rushing around recording their visit there. Phones were used extensively to record the scene. No doubt these captured photos would soon be uploaded for many others to enjoy; or maybe just to see. The most popular shot seemed to be a selfie with the Dome of the Rock in the background. Tablets and iPads were also being held aloft to capture a lasting record. Only one member of the group appeared to be a serious photographer. Hanging over his shoulder was a bright, blue camera bag and around his neck hung an impressive SLR Canon.

This was Colin Foster. He would seize on every photo opportunity and was continually changing lenses from his over-sized bag to achieve the best possible outcome. 'After my wife died,' he had explained to Gordon, 'I took up photography. People think I'm a nut, but it has really made my life easier since her death.'

Soon enough photographs had been taken and sufficient maps of Jerusalem purchased. It was time to move on. It was time to leave the lookout point with its beautifully paved areas and limestone banks of seating. It was time to follow in Jesus' footsteps down Palm Sunday Road. Time to walk down that road to the next scheduled stop.

Then the man with a donkey appeared. He was encouraging the visitors to have their photo taken with his beast. For a price.

'Here's a thought,' Tony addressed Pastor Paul. 'Jesus spent his working life walking around the countryside with his disciples, preaching and teaching. Right?'

'Yes,' agreed the Pastor, 'he was an itinerant preacher and teacher, and most would have the idea that he walked everywhere.'

'But then,' continued Tony, 'he arrives at the Mount of Olives, the doorstep of his destination, Jerusalem, just a couple of ks to go, and what does he decide to do? He decides to ride that last little stretch on a donkey.'

A few others had gathered around and were wondering where this conversation was heading. The Pastor's wife, Julie, had to remind everyone that Jesus did that to fulfil an Old Testament prophesy.

But Tony ignored her and continued, 'And it's a pretty steep pinch down into the valley from up here. And it was probably steeper then. It would have been much easier walking down the path than balancing on a small donkey while it picked its way between the rocks and ruts.'

Colin was putting his camera back into one of the compartments in his camera case while he joined in the conversation. 'I don't think it was a last-minute decision when he chose to ride a donkey down the hill. It is clear that he had this planned a long time ahead. The story reads like a real spy thriller. You even have the locals demanding a password from the two men Jesus sent to collect the animal.'

'You're right,' agreed Tony. 'And then one of the Gospel writers... Matthew, did you say Pastor...? Well Matthew has Jesus riding on the donkey and her colt. Was he doing some sort of circus trick.'

'I think you are taking things a little bit too far,' said Pastor Paul rather sternly.

At this point Sarah arrived and the conversation stopped. She pointed to the Australian flag held aloft some twenty metres ahead. 'We all better keep moving,' she said politely. 'I would hate to lose anyone on the very first morning. Jesus apparently rode down here on a donkey. You unfortunately will have to walk.'

\* \* \*

## Extract from Andrew's travel diary:

> We arrived at the Mount of Olives. I looked and saw a hillside paved in gravestones.
> Oh people, Oh dwellers in this Holy Land,
> What have you done to the Mount of Olives?
> Oh you people.
> You have rooted out that growing green which was life,
> which gave sustenance to life.
> You have laid bare here the slopes of this mount of deep meaning.
> Oh people.
> You have sacrificed the living for the dead.
> That which encouraged life, lived life,
> now lies useless, lifeless,

suppressed by the stones of the dead.
People, Oh you people.
Let the soil bring forth.
Do not hinder it.
Let the earth join in the joy of creation.
Do not deny it.
Oh people
Let the Mount live its life.
Do not deny it!
Join with it and sing with it.
Learn once again to rejoice in it.

*A teardrop shaped finial: a feature on the Chapel of Dominus Flevit located on Palm Sunday Road descending from the Mount of Olives. Here Jesus wept.*

Chapter 3

# Triumphant Entry

JERUSALEM, 36 CE:

All roads were leading to Jerusalem and they were crowded. The Passover festival was only a week away and Jewish people from far and near were on their way to be part of the ceremonies and celebrations. From Egypt and Libya they came, from Arabia and Mesopotamia, from Pontus, Phrygia and Pamphylia, from Rome and the Mediterranean. Most however were from the outer regions of Judea and distant Galilee. The streams were slowly approaching their pilgrimage goal. Jews and converts to Judaism were heading to the Holy City to celebrate once more God's compassion in rescuing their ancestors from slavery in Egypt.

This year the crowds were even larger than normal, swollen particularly by local pilgrims from Judea and Galilee. The country had just experienced a Jubilee Year, when according to tradition the land was to be rested, the fields left fallow. This would happen every seven years. As a result, the required workforce was less, and more had the opportunity to attend the Passover festivities. It also meant that more had less income to feed themselves and their children.

To make matters worse for the local peasants, 35 CE had been a Roman census year for the purpose of organising the compulsory tax which was required by the Emperor. This was held every fourteen years. The time had now arrived for the tax to be collected and this caused heightened resentment, not only towards the Roman overlords but also towards the tax collectors. The talk in the towns and on the roads was about taxes and tax collectors.

These were volatile times when a gifted orator or leader could easily incite the disgruntled crowds to unwise actions. The Roman authorities were well aware of this situation and would arrange special precautions at Passover time.

Ultimate governing power in the Jewish homeland was concentrated in the hands of the Roman Emperor who at this time was Tiberius. At the local level it resided in his appointed representative, the Governor Pontius Pilate.

Pilate resided in his palace in Caesarea Maritima situated on the Mediterranean coast. The climate and general environment here were preferable to that in the capital city located in the hills inland. At the times of the major festivals he would come up to Jerusalem. This was not because of any religious fervour, after all he was a Roman. He came up with military reinforcements to be close on hand to deal with any trouble which might erupt. With many thousands of citizens arriving in the already crowded city and knowing from experience the discontent under which the people lived, he knew that it would only take a spark to start a nasty anti-government protest.

Pilate embodied locally all that the Emperor Tiberius represented. This included not only the power of civic government but also the notion of imperial theology in which Tiberius was to be worshipped as the Son of God. Pilate's entry into the city of Jerusalem was a display of this might, and also a reminder of the divine attributes of the Emperor and the reverence with which he was to be honoured.

With the Passover festival a mere week away, Governor Pontius Pilate and his entourage were approaching Jerusalem. His entry would send a clear message to the citizens of this Holy

City, as well as to the many visitors, that Roman power was not to be underestimated.

The drum corps announced the approach of marching feet. Members of the Governor's personal security unit marched tall and proud, strictly in time to the echoing beat of the drums. The unevenness of the cobblestone street could not be used as an excuse for a stumbling foot. The colourful uniforms of the legionnaires surged forward with their helmets and weapons glittering in the spring sunshine. The heads of the soldiers were held high. The banners and insignias were also held aloft, designed to flutter in the breeze. Today they drooped limply.

The governmental procession marched through the Gennath Gate into the city of Jerusalem. The local citizens lining the street witnessing this Roman display of power, this triumphant entry, stood with heads bowed low. There were no shouts of goodwill. There were no cheers of welcome. Most showed the brooding resignation of a subservient people. Some looked up with active anger in their eyes. Others caressed the daggers which they carried, hidden beneath the folds of their cloaks. 'The time will come,' they were thinking, 'when the proud arrogance marching along the streets of our Holy City would feel the sharp edges of these daggers, the cold stab of resistance.'

What excitement would this Passover week bring? Would this be the year for a concerted effort to rid the country of the Roman overlords? Would those committed to armed resistance be ready to come forward should the word be given? Would a leader arise to give this word?

.................................................................................

Andrew and Tony were sitting under an olive tree in the grounds of the Chapel of Dominus Flevit. Tony was still wiping his mouth trying to get rid of the taste of the purple olive which he had picked from above his head. They were half way down the narrow, rather steep asphalt road that is today known as Palm Sunday Road.

After waiting for Tony to conclude a colourful description of the olive which he had just tasted, Andrew said, 'Imagine you were there.' He was trying to take Tony back to Mark's account of Jesus' entry into Jerusalem prior to his arrest and crucifixion. The account had been read earlier by a member of the group to set the biblical scene of their present location.

Mark's account was still fresh in his mind and he had been sitting trying to visualise the procession. With hosannas ringing in his ears he saw the Galilee preacher man sitting astride a tired-looking donkey. But the enthusiasm of the crowd around him added another dimension to the scene. 'Blessed is the kingdom of our father David that is coming,' they had been shouting. Clearly, they were expecting great things. What exactly were they expecting?

'But we were there!' Tony's reply indicated that he was still in the present and hadn't taken himself back 2000 years as his friend had meant him to do. He continued before Andrew had a chance to say anything, 'We're in the middle of it all. I waited at the side of the road as a younger, more energetic group of pilgrims to ours, hurried their descent. I waited to the side as another group made its way up the road. I made way for taxis and other vehicles which had every right to be on this particular street. I waited as members of our group needed to make a comfort stop. I looked in amazement — while I was standing on the side of the road waiting — at the endless rows of Jewish tombstones with pebbles on top of them that stretched away in the distance. I kept my eyes open for the Lord, but he seemed to be long gone from this pathway. His footprints have been paved over with modern technology. They had been trampled underfoot by the many thousands, or perhaps millions, of pilgrims who were here searching, listening for his words of comfort and assurance, awaiting his faith-strengthening messages.'

Andrew was frustrated. 'No, you silly beggar! You know what I mean. You really carry on when you get going, don't you? Imagine you were here, back then. Back in the scene described by Mark and the other evangelists.'

'Oh, back then!' said an innocent-looking Tony, feigning miscomprehension. 'Now I see what you mean. Which me do you want back there? Do you want me there as one of the twelve disciples, a follower or just an idle bystander? Or maybe, perhaps, the 21st century me who is a fan of Dr Who?'

'Trust you to make things complicated,' Andrew was becoming exasperated. 'No, not a 21st century you. And I can't imagine Jesus would have picked you as one of his special disciples. You're certainly not a good fisherman.'

'Hold on,' interrupted Tony. 'Now who's being facetious? Let's say that I'm just an idle bystander.'

'Fine. Now what would you be thinking?'

'Well now, let me think,' replied Tony. 'I would wonder what sort of a pantomime these visitors are putting on. They are obviously out-of-towners who have come for the Passover celebrations. There is this ordinary-looking man riding on a sad-looking donkey and the people are treating him like a king. Are they serious or are they having him on? They are shouting out inappropriate phrases which seem to come from our Holy Writings. They are putting tree branches and their cloaks on the path for him to ride over. And the noise! I would be wondering what this was all about.'

'So, it wouldn't be clear to you what was happening? What all the cheering was about?' prompted Andrew.

'No, not really, unless I went to ask someone. But I would

make sure to keep well clear of the whole procession. If the authorities got word of what was happening here, there would be hell to pay. The soldiers are very trigger happy at Passover time especially with all these crowds around.'

'You wouldn't see this man on the donkey as a god then?'

'Good heavens, no,' replied Tony. 'There is only one god and he doesn't go riding around on a donkey. I would have learnt that as a child. But as I said, I would have kept well away. Probably hidden behind that bougainvillea bush over there.'

It was out of the biblical description of this event that the Christian commemoration of Palm Sunday was born. But this title did not arise from Mark's writing (*leafy branches which they had cut from the fields*), nor from Matthew's (*others cut branches from the trees*), nor Luke who has no mention of any kind of vegetation. Only in John's Gospel are palm branches mentioned. In modern parlance, they rolled out the red carpet for this special dignitary.

The two were so occupied with their discussion that they were unaware that the tour guide, Sarah, had approached them.

'Hello. You two seem to be having a very serious conversation, but it's now time to keep moving. Now, let me see. You're Andrew Wagner, right?' she said looking towards Anthony.

'No, bad guess,' said Tony. 'I'm actually the good-looking one, Anthony. But you can call me Tony. That would be Andrew right here beside me.'

'Oh, I'm sorry. But I do like to get to know the people in my group. As I said on the bus this morning, please call me Sarah. And I am pleased to meet you, Anthony. Or should I say Tony? And you also Andrew. I hope I won't confuse you next time.'

With that they joined the other members of the group and were soon following the Australian flag, held high, fluttering against a background of purple bougainvillea.

And people were getting to know one another as they walked along. Members of this group soon realised that the person walking beside them, or closely behind or in front of them, was not really a stranger but someone who had chosen to come on this pilgrimage to Israel; another Christian. This presented many doorways for striking up a conversation.

Sarah had gone off to round up some more stragglers and Andrew and Tony joined the flow behind two couples who were making themselves known to one another.

'Tell me, what did you think about that place? The Dominus Flevit Chapel?' asked one woman of the couple beside her.

'Yes, Dominus Flevit. Jesus wept. It's a pity we couldn't get inside to have a look round. By the way, I'm Stephen. Stephen Gersekowski and my wife, Frances.'

'Sorry for being so rude. We are Gary and Judith Waller,' said Judith. 'But yes, I suppose it won't be the last time we don't get to see everything. That's what I said to Gary when we were deciding to come. Hope there aren't crowds of people everywhere.'

Frances joined in the conversation. 'Nice to meet you, Judith and Gary. It was Gary, wasn't it? Yes, I checked out most of the places we were to visit on the net over the last few months. It would have been nice to see inside for the actual thing is always more interesting than just looking at pictures of it.'

'If you want to know anything about where we are going, just ask Frances,' said her husband Stephen. 'She certainly has come prepared. I rather just take things as I find them.'

'Gary likes to prepare too,' said Judith, 'but more so by studying the Bible references about each place we are to visit. He was very keen to come here much more than me. I'm a bit like you, Stephen. I am... how can I say it...? sort of spontaneous. I'll enjoy them when I see them.'

'I know exactly what you are saying,' Stephen replied. 'So

often reality does not live up to what was expected. One can be a little disappointed.'

'What I find interesting,' said Gary, after listening quietly to the others, 'is how they have taken some comment of Jesus and made it into a pilgrim site. Luke says in his Gospel that Jesus wept over the city of Jerusalem. He doesn't say exactly where Jesus may have done that, only as he approached Jerusalem.'

'So it could have been anywhere?' suggested Frances.

'Well, not really. Luke has it between Jesus' triumphant entry and his visiting the temple. So I suppose this was as good a place as any around here. Sarah did say that it was built over some old remains.'

Then Frances continued, 'Yes, I read about that as well. There must have been some tradition concerning this site. I suppose the exact spot is not so important really. Just so that we are reminded of Jesus' love and care for people.'

'That's a good way of looking at it,' said Gary. 'I know we couldn't get inside the building because of the service being held there but I did like the outside. Especially those teardrop-shaped finials on the four corner pillars. I shall remember it as teardrops from heaven.' Gary kept talking to Frances about his impression of the chapel.

They had begun their conversation walking four abreast but as the conversation continued and because of the oncoming crush of people they formed into two pairs walking behind one another. The two wives, Frances and Judith, did not end up walking together as is often the case when two couples meet. Stephen and Gary's wife, Judith, went ahead commenting on the fruit stall which they had just passed and its wonderful display of produce. The other two were discussing the ossuaries displayed in the garden of the Dominus Flevit Chapel.

Chapter 4

# Shepherds' Field

The world — mainly the Christian world — has the evangelist St Luke to thank for recording the remarkable events which took place in the fields outside Bethlehem on the evening of Jesus' birth. He writes (Luke 2: 8-16):

> *And there were shepherds living out in the fields nearby, keeping watch over their flocks at night. An angel of the Lord appeared to them, and the glory of the Lord shone around them, and they were terrified. But the angel said to them, "Do not be afraid. I bring you good news of great joy that will be for all the people. Today in the town of David a saviour has been born to you; he is Christ the Lord. This will be a sign to you: You will find a baby wrapped in clothes and lying in a manger."*
>
> *Suddenly a great company of the heavenly host appeared with the angel, praising God and saying, "Glory to God in the highest, and on earth peace to men on whom his favour rests."*
>
> *When the angels had left them and gone into heaven, the shepherds said to one another, "Let's go to Bethlehem and see this thing that has happened, which the Lord has told us about." So they hurried off and found Mary and Joseph, and the baby, who was lying in the manger.*

Neither Mark nor John have included birth details of Jesus in their Gospels. It is Matthew and Luke who have given the world details on which present-day Christmas pageants are based.

Their accounts, when considered separately, seem to vary considerably in content and tone and the version which is heard and seen today is usually an amalgam of both with some traditional, non-biblical details included.

Luke's account, part of which is the account of the angels' visit to the shepherds quoted above, emphasises the excitement and happiness of the situation. His is an account which reflects similar sentiments to that of Isaac Watts when he wrote some 1700 years later: *Joy to the world, the Lord is come*. Although it's thought that he wrote his Christmas carol with Psalm 98 in mind, there is no doubt that his verses reflect the celebratory mood that is found in Luke. After all Christmas should be a happy time, celebrating a birthday.

Luke's account of Jesus' birth is free of the dark and gloom which characterises Matthew's version. There is no intrigue surrounding the visit of some oriental dignitaries, no royal anger, no slaughtering of innocent children. The Christ child and his parents do not need to flee as refugees to a foreign country to escape death. Luke has heaven rejoicing at the birth of Jesus and sharing this mood with the shepherds near Bethlehem. It is his account that brings the many bus loads of pilgrims to this location.

The bus bearing the Australian flag pulled up at the front entrance to the Franciscan site which remembers the shepherds' encounter with the heavenly hosts. The happy passengers poured out and headed for the entrance arch which certainly had a biblical, Christmassy ring about it. **Gloria in excelsis deo** was written boldly and cheerfully in bright red on the arch (Glory to God in the highest, from Luke 2:14).

The Gersekowskis and Wallers, after having met on Palm Sunday Road, found themselves together again after alighting from the bus. Although from different states in Australia they found that they had common acquaintances. The fact that they were of similar age and religious background also helped to make conversation flow easily. The more they chatted the more it became evident that they had similar interests.

Gary Waller with his love of Bible study and Stephen's wife, Frances, who was fascinated by interesting details of Biblical sites, were soon involved in a religious discussion. Frances was explaining how she had found that the Franciscan site they were now visiting was not the only chapel dedicated to the shepherds. There was also a Greek Orthodox Monastery which commemorated the night of Jesus' birth.

Their partners, Judy and Stephen, had less interest in such discussions and were generally happy to talk about their own interests — football, friends, food and fun.

Andrew and Tony were walking beside Pastor Paul and his wife commenting on what they at first expected on their trip to Israel.

'You know,' began Andrew, 'when Gordon contacted me with his generous offer and I first started thinking seriously about coming here, I had no idea of what we might be seeing. I hadn't ever thought about it for it was never on my bucket list. Actually, I have never had a so-called bucket list!'

'Yes, I know what you mean,' said Julie, the Pastor's wife. 'When Paul first told me that Gordon had asked him whether he would be interested in going and being the spiritual leader for the group, I immediately began looking to see what we might be visiting.'

Tony then joined in. 'I too, never had any intentions of doing the pilgrim thing here. Then when Andrew asked me to help him I didn't have much time to think about it. No doubt we would be visiting the obvious places like Jerusalem, the Sea of Galilee, Bethlehem, Nazareth and perhaps Cana. That's about as far as my thinking went.'

'Then when the itinerary arrived, and I looked at it seriously in detail, I was somewhat surprised at the list of places we would be visiting,' continued Andrew. 'Such places as the Church of the Multiplication of the Loaves and Fishes, Mount of the Leap, the House of Simon the Potter and this place, the Shepherds' Field, never entered my mind. Sure, they are biblical references I am aware of, but to give them a specific geographical location, to place these events on a map, this I was not expecting.'

'I can understand your thinking completely,' said Pastor Paul. 'Here we are however, in the middle of it all. Well we are near the Palestinian town of Bethlehem, which you thought we would have to be visiting. But to be visiting the Shepherds' Field! I can see it must have been a surprise.'

They had passed under the welcoming arch and were walking along a wide path paved in pale limestone rectangles. A number of simply-designed garden seats were positioned along the pathway encouraging the visitors to sit and meditate or merely sit and rest. Ahead, a small limestone building was highlighted by a backdrop of dark green foliage; pine trees, palms and cedars.

This was the Barluzzi-designed chapel which showed echoes of the tents of the nomadic herders of previous centuries, less noticeable in the twenty-first. An angel over the front entrance welcomed the visitors and brought to mind Luke's Angel of the Lord which appeared to the shepherds. Above this depiction were positioned three arches containing bells ready to ring out their welcome of joy.

Three low steps transported the visitors from the dusty limestone pavers into the presence of ancient shepherds and heavenly hosts. The interior was colourfully decorated with scenes of angels, shepherds with their sheep and mosaics depicting appropriate nativity scenes. The light that beamed through the circular glass panels in the ceiling was a more subtle reminder of the light (the Glory of God, Luke 2:9) that shone about the shepherds on that eventful evening.

It was this interior that created the right atmosphere to hear once again St Luke's account of the shepherds' experience and to sing a couple of Christmas carols. Pastor Paul explained that the reading had to come from St Luke and not St Mark, his favourite Gospel, for, as he put it, 'there are no Christmas trees in Mark's Gospel'. The party agreed that although it may have theoretically been the wrong time of year to sing Christmas carols, in this chapel any time of year would be the right time.

With the last stanza of *While shepherds watched their flocks by night* completed, Sarah made the announcement to move back to the bus. 'Just like the shepherds which you have been singing about,' she said, 'we also must now move off to Bethlehem to see the baby. Well not exactly the baby; but the place where he was born.'

'Will we actually see some shepherds and their flocks here in the fields?' someone wanted to know. 'I didn't notice any as we were walking along the path.'

'No. At this time of year,' Sarah explained, 'you will only see dry, hungry fields with beds of pale limestone making it difficult for the struggling grass to find a footing. The sheep are being grazed elsewhere. Grass will come when the rain arrives, and the sheep will be back then. But we can't wait for that. The bus will leave in thirty minutes.'

Andrew and Tony were walking along with a couple of ladies whom they had not yet really met. They had briefly talked to Andrew on the Mount of Olives.

'Oh, I'm so excited,' gushed Margaret Schneider. 'I just can't express how I feel. Just imagine. Two thousand years ago angels came down from heaven and spoke to the shepherds on this exact spot. Isn't it wonderful that we are now here singing to the Lord like those heavenly hosts back then?'

The boys were a little taken aback by the religious fervour and enthusiasm of this woman, and they didn't quite know how to respond. Andrew looked at his friend, hoping that there would be no response coming from him. He knew how Tony felt about those who, in his mind, were too religious. He also knew from experience that he was not backward in making his feeling known.

Tony had stopped and was looking at the two women ready to speak. Andrew held his breath and his hand clamped hard on the small camera case he was carrying.

Tony began. 'I think it's great, Mrs ... I'm sorry, I don't know your name.'

'It's Mrs Schneider. Margaret Schneider. And you are Andrew, aren't you?'

'No, sorry Mrs Schneider. I'm Tony. This is Andrew, the quiet one of us,' he said, pointing to his friend. 'But as I was about to say. It's great that you can be so uplifted by our visit here. I suppose that's what going on a pilgrimage to the Holy Land like this is all about, and not just looking at the sights.'

Margaret smiled her agreement and then turned to Andrew. 'And how have you found the day so far, Andrew?'

'I... Oh well...' stumbled Andrew recovering from his amazement at his friend's comments, 'I... ah... yes... the surprises keep coming.' And he noticed Tony smiling. 'To tell you the truth. I'm having trouble keeping up with everything.'

'Oh, I'm sorry to hear that. I heard someone saying that there was a young man in the group who had some medical problems. I take it that's you. Has this first day been a little too strenuous for you?'

'No, it's not that,' replied Andrew. 'I'm having trouble digesting all of the factual information they keep throwing at me.'

'I know exactly what you mean,' said Margaret's companion.

'Oh, and I'm Avril Baumgartner. Margaret here and I go back a long time. We met in Springwood as teenagers, and…'

'I think you mean Springbrook, don't you Avril?' interrupted Margaret.

'Springbrook. Yes, that's what I meant,' corrected Avril. 'We were both up there with our families on holiday. We really live in Victoria. We've heard so much today that I'm all confused. And the day isn't finished yet.'

They were approaching the entrance arch on leaving the site and straight ahead printed large on a building stood *Bo'az Field Souvenir Shop* to which some members of the group were hastening. A little further down the road was a sign to *Ruth's Field Restaurant*.

Tony called the signs to the attention of Andrew and the two ladies accompanying them. 'Hey! Look at those signs there. Bo'az Field and Ruth's Field. It looks as though more than our good shepherds are laying claim to these fields.'

'What could that mean? Do you have any idea, Margaret?' Avril asked her friend.

'Ruth, yes. That's a short book in the Old Testament,' she replied. 'It's squeezed between Judges and Samuel. I can never find it when I want to and usually have to look up the page number in the index at the beginning of the Bible. And you remember the story of Ruth and her mother-in-law Naomi, don't you Avril?'

'Oh, yes. There is that bit about where you go I will go and where you stay I will stay, but that's about all I know about Ruth. And as for Bo'az. I've never really heard of him.'

Tony came to the rescue. 'Ruth and her mother-in-law came back home here to Bethlehem. Bo'az was a wealthy cousin of Naomi living here and she arranged for Ruth to seduce him… '

Andrew butted in. 'I think that's enough detail for the moment, Tony. You will only confuse the issue even further.

Say, why don't we leave the ladies and have a quick look in that souvenir shop?'

With a 'catch you later' they left the two confused ladies and joined the others making their way to buy some reminders of their visit here.

## Chapter 5

# Bethlehem

In the middle of the nineteenth century, Rector Phillip Brooks of Philadelphia took a pilgrimage tour to the Holy Land. The memories of his time there were such that on his return to America he was moved to compose a poem. It began:

*O little town of Bethlehem*
*How still we see thee lie,*
*Beneath thy deep and dreamless sleep*
*The silent stars go by.*

It is clear that the rector was very impressed with the peacefulness and serenity of Bethlehem as he experienced it. His poem became a well-loved Christmas carol. In the weeks leading up to Christmas the words and music can be heard on the radio and TV, in shopping malls and in churches throughout countries with a Christian heritage.

More than two and a half thousand years earlier, a local prophet, Micah, also made reference to this town. He wrote:

*But you, Bethlehem, Ephrathah,*
*though you are small among the clans of Judah,*
*out of you will come for me*
*one who will be ruler over Israel,*
*whose origins are from old, from ancient times (Micah 5:2).*

This was written in uncertain times when Assyrian forces were overrunning Judah, and Bethlehem was a town which could easily be conquered. It was not an important town at that time and probably the peace and serenity which Rector Brooks experienced was not there either, shattered by the prospect of being overrun by an advancing enemy army.

Later, Jewish writers saw these words of Micah as a prophecy that the long-awaited Jewish Messiah would be born in this town. As a result, we have Matthew in his gospel describing how Joseph and Mary, who according to him were residents there living in their own home, had a child whom they named Jesus. On the other hand, Luke in his Gospel, had Joseph and Mary coming south from their hometown of Nazareth in Galilee to Bethlehem to fill in their census forms. While here, Mary gave birth to her first child, Jesus. These two biblical writers, Matthew and Luke, firmly established the village of Bethlehem as the place where Jesus was born. People are still journeying to this place, today more than ever, to see for themselves this town. In particular they come to stand on the very spot where the child was born, assuming that this can be determined.

Like the shepherds of old, Gordon Lange's group of Aussie pilgrims also made their way to Bethlehem to meditate on Jesus' birth, with its geographic setting adding greatly to the experience. Unlike Rector Brooks, who remembered the "silent stars" of his evening visit, they were there in the midday warmth of a clear October day, and his "little town" had grown into a scattered, in parts untidy, city of many thousands of people.

Their focus, however, was not on its size or appearance or the local weather report but on the Church of the Nativity, one of the most visited pilgrim sites in the Holy Land. According to tradition, this old basilica was built over the place where Jesus was born. To be more exact, the present building was built on the remains of a previous church built over the cave where Jesus was born.

The group had wandered through this old Basilica, glancing around in wonder at the ancient building. They had watched as priests from the Armenian Christian Church performed their daily rituals and had then taken the steps to a lower level. They were deep within the bowels of the earth — that was how Margaret Schneider put it as she caught up with Pastor Paul. Although everyone had been introduced at the welcome dinner the night before, many in the group did not know one another at this early stage of the tour. Pastor Paul was one of the exceptions. Because tour leader, Gordon, introduced him in connection with his special role as tour Chaplain, everyone remembered him. People with questions relating to their Christian faith and beliefs could turn to him.

'We came here to see where the Christ Child was born and ended up in a cave,' Margaret came straight to the point. 'If I rightly remember from my Sunday School days Jesus was born in a stable attached to an inn. Isn't that right?' she directed her question to Pastor Paul.

'Yes,' he replied, 'I'm sure that's what you would have learnt.'

Before he could say anything further, Margaret continued, 'We had to learn Bible verses by heart back then. How many young children have to do that today? I still remember pieces from our Christmas program. "And she brought forth her first born son and wrapped him in swaddling clothes and laid him in a manger, because there was no room for them in the inn." That's what I learnt then. No mention of a cave there!'

Margate's friend, Avril, had caught up to them by this time and agreed with her friend's memory. 'Yes,' she said, 'I remember learning that too. Pastor Schirmann insisted that we learn it by heart.'

'I think you mean Pastor Riemann, don't you Avril?' prompted Margaret.

'Oh, yes, it was Pastor Riemann,' corrected Avril. 'So, what do you think, Pastor Paul? I'm confused like Margaret.'

'I can understand your confusion,' replied Pastor Paul, 'but I don't think we can discuss it on the run here. Or should I say on the walk?'

'No, probably not,' said Margaret. 'And Sarah said that we need to hurry on and sit down in the cave up ahead. But I'll tell you something, Pastor, tradition or no tradition, I'll stick to my belief that he was born in a stable behind an inn.'

'And I won't disagree with you,' added Avril.

Members of the group had all heard the message, told to them in the Church of the Nativity, that Jesus was born in a cave. They had also seen the altar and the star in a cave which commemorated the birth. There were many others in this party, besides Margaret and Avril, who heard and saw with surprise and scepticism. They, as of yet, had not made their feelings known to Pastor Paul or Gordon.

The first church built here was constructed by Emperor Constantine the Great. It was mainly his mother, Helena, who travelled widely throughout the Holy Land locating places which had reference to the life of Jesus. According to the information she tracked down, Jesus was born in a cave here in Bethlehem. So in 327 CE Constantine had a church built over the cave to preserve the site for posterity.

This original church was burnt down in 550 CE, but a replacement was built over the site fifteen years later. It is this sixth century church, with various renovations, which can still be visited today. It is one of the oldest churches in the Holy Land.

Visitors are directed to enter through the very low front door, the Door of Humility, walk up the aisle to the main altar, then down the steps into an underground cave. There under an altar, the Altar of Nativity, is a silver star. This marks the spot where Jesus was born. But a CAVE? What about the stable one sees in all the nativity scenes which pop up in the months before Christmas?

Where was he born? A stable or a cave? That is the question. Matthew seems to indicate that Jesus was born in Joseph and Mary's home which was located in Bethlehem, for when the Magi arrived looking for him 18-24 months after his birth they came to *the house where they saw the child with his mother Mary* (Matthew 2:11). Luke on the other hand says that Joseph and Mary were visitors from Nazareth in distant Galilee and couldn't find a place to lodge. Mary felt labour pains beginning. Where could she go? She and Joseph found what protection they could and after the child was born the only suitable place to lay him down was in a manger which was there. Luke writes: *She wrapped him in cloths and placed him in a manger, because there was no room for them in the inn* (Luke 2:7). And later, the sign given to the shepherds by the angel of the Lord was that they would *find a baby wrapped in cloths and lying in a manger* (Luke 2:12).

These two references of Luke are responsible for the generally held impression that Jesus was born in a stable behind an inn. Here is just one of the many confusions which surround the birth of Jesus. Luke does not say that it was in a stable, simply that Mary lay the baby in a manger. Neither Matthew nor Luke can answer the question of whether Jesus was born in a cave or a stable. Indeed, there are biblical scholars today who say that he was born in neither, not even in Bethlehem but probably in a house in Nazareth.

The written indication that the birth place was in a cave goes back a long way. Justin Martyr, born around 100 CE, writes in a book entitled *Dialogue with Trypho*: *But when the Child was born in Bethlehem, since Joseph could not find a lodging in that village, he took up his quarters in a certain cave near the village; and while they were there Mary brought forth the Christ and placed him in a manger.*

Biblical scholars argue one way or the other. So do the visitors who come to the Church of the Nativity. Some may have had their minds changed by a visit here; others not.

\* \* \*

EXTRACT FROM ANDREW'S TRAVEL DIARY:

And so what about my personal visit to this traditional site of the birth of Jesus? Well, it left me all a little confused and, I must say, not spiritually uplifted because of my time there. My main memory of the Church of the Nativity is the small (low) entrance door. It is easy to see where the name Door of Humility came from. One really has to bow low when entering the building. Inside can be seen the old stone work which outlined the original entrance — much larger and grander. We were told that the entrance had been purposely lowered so that horsemen were not able to ride their steeds into the church. True or another urban myth? Who knows?

And the cave in which the Altar of the Nativity covering the fourteen-pointed star was situated was very crowded with people eager to stoop down and photograph or kiss the star and meditate on the birth of the Lord. It was nearing the end of a long and tiring day during which many holy sites had been visited, and unfortunately this place did not receive the attention from me which it merited. The church next door awaited with its own caves and stories.

And let's face it. Most Christians are quite happy with the nativity scene we are used to seeing today. This is the one in which as many of the elements mentioned by Matthew and Luke (and some not mentioned by them) are crowded in and around a stable. We must not let the true facts (if indeed they can ever be discerned) stand in the way of this romanticised popular version which is Christmas for most Christian communities.

If I get the opportunity I must ask Sarah what she thinks. Someone mentioned that she was a Jew, so she might have a different insight. I think she has more than good looks, something which Tony noticed right away.

*Wall painting inside the Barluzzi-designed Shepherds' Field Chapel near Bethlehem.*

## Chapter 6

# Jerome

Facing the Manger Square and butting hard against the Church of the Nativity in Bethlehem is the Roman Catholic Church of St Catherine. The network of caves found under the Church of the Nativity extends under this church as well. It made tour-guide sense to move from Jesus' birth cave directly to other points of interest within this underground network of rooms. After the range of reactions expressed while visiting Jesus' birthplace concluded, the group had made its way to a cave set up with a number of seats. Here weary bones could be rested, and minds given time to digest what they had just experienced and prepare for the next onslaught of information, explanations and interpretations.

After a few sundry remarks Sarah explained the purpose of their present stop. She began, 'I'm sure you are all enjoying sitting down for a rest but while in Bethlehem we need also to remember St Jerome, an important name in the annals of early Christian history. A tall statue of him stands in front of this church above us. If you look you will see that the name on the plinth is … wait a moment,' at this point she looked at her book of notes, 'yes, S. HIERONYMUS. That name wouldn't mean much to most people. Hieronymus was the name given at his birth, but he is best remembered as St Jerome.

'Why is he remembered? He was one of the great writers of the early Christian Church, but remembered mainly for his translation into Latin of our Hebrew Scriptures, or as you know it, the Old Testament. His translation which became known as the Vulgate was the Bible of choice for the Roman Catholic Church for centuries.

'In 388 CE, at the age of forty, he came to Israel and spent the rest of his life, some 32 years, living in a cave here in Bethlehem. It is generally accepted he lived and worked in one of the caves in this complex here beneath the Church of St Catherine. He chose this place for, as tradition has it, and as you have just been told, Jesus was born in a cave here as well.

'Here he devoted the last years of his life to translating and writing religious works. The Old Testament used at that time was the Septuagint, a Greek translation compiled a few centuries before the Common Era. He chose to make his Latin translation from the Hebrew original which he claimed was the inspired text, and not from the Greek version in common use. For fifteen years he devoted himself to this task. After he completed the Bible translation he spent the rest of his life writing books condemning heresies which had arisen and commentaries on various books of the Bible.

'Although he lived in a cave, maybe even this one, he was not a hermit who cut himself off from the rest of the world. He did have a group of friends who accompanied him from Rome and offered support, both financial and personal. The mosaic picture behind the altar in the cave next to us here depicts Jerome and three of his friends. To his right is St Paula, a rich widow from Rome who provided financial support. The other two are St Eustochium, Paula's daughter, and St Eusebius. You can have a good look at this when we move out.

'As we are now discovering, caves can provide a cool retreat from the summer heat of Israel. It was quite warm outside but here the temperature is very agreeable. In the days before air-conditioning this would have been an advantage. Then in winter when it became a little chilly in the cave, wood-burning stoves would have provided warmth. In other words, living in a cave was not as primitive as it might seem to us.

'But that's enough from me. I now have a surprise for you. I am going to ask Colin Foster to come up here and talk to you about... No, I'll let him explain.'

Colin was a tall, quiet man. Shortly after retiring from the accounting business where he had worked for many years, his wife suddenly died. For many months he was lost and found it difficult to face the future alone. Finally, his daughter persuaded him to go on one of those trips he and his wife had been planning. This was the beginning of his love of travelling, albeit now alone, and photography. Now, loaded down with his camera cases and full of pre-travel, googled information he was here in a cave in Bethlehem enjoying his pilgrimage to the Holy Land. He quietly, shyly, moved to the front of the expectant group.

He began. 'My standing up here is probably a good example of what might happen if you put your hand up instead of sitting on it. Now I am suffering and soon you will probably be suffering as well but I hope not too badly.

'Some months ago, Sarah here, and our leader Gordon, were meeting with a group of us in Brisbane telling us about this tour. At one stage Sarah showed us a photograph of a sculpture and asked if anyone knew what it was. Silly me put up my hand and that's what landed me here in front of you.'

Colin smiled as someone asked, 'Well what was it Colin? What was the photo all about?'

'It was a photo of one of Michelangelo's sculptures called Moses. But a very interesting sculpture.'

'But what does Moses or Michelangelo have to do with Bethlehem?' The same person had interrupted.

'I hope I'll soon get round to that. But bear with me. I am an old accountant and approach things very slowly.'

'No, it doesn't add up.' This came from Andrew's friend, Tony. There was a scattering of laughter at this comment, but it didn't stop Andrew giving Tony a dig in the ribs and saying, 'Let him get on with it.'

Colin smiled, looked at the notes he was holding in his hand and continued. 'The sculpture is regarded as one of Michelangelo's masterpieces This in itself makes it a must-see but an intriguing aspect of this work is how he has portrayed Moses. He has depicted Moses with two horns growing out of the top of his head. This is the famous horned Moses.' At this point Colin looked up at his audience and on seeing a number of puzzled brows commented, 'Judging by the look on many faces, probably not so famous! However, it was a work of art that I was finally able to visit, after wanting to see it for a number of years.

'You are perhaps wondering why I was so interested? Well, this was in itself a long journey. Where did it begin? Probably when I was reading an article about mistranslations and errors which have occurred in various translations of the Bible. It was suggested somewhere I read that St Jerome's translation of Exodus 34:29 in the Latin Vulgate Bible was incorrect. That is what gets us here to this cave.

'He wrote that when Moses came down from the mountain after receiving the two tablets of the law from the Lord God his face was horned.' Here Colin looked at his notes again and continued, 'For those of you who understand Latin, *cornuta esset facies sua*. What, none of you? The Septuagint, which as Sarah had explained was a Greek translation of the Old Testament which had been in use for centuries, had stated that the skin on Moses face was radiating, not that he had horns. Thus, Jerome's translation seemed to be at odds with the recognised version.

'This started me off on research into what various scholars had to say on the subject. My searches inevitability led me to

Michelangelo's horned Moses which was a famous rendition of St Jerome's "error". So, last year when I knew that my Mediterranean cruise of the Greek Islands would terminate in Rome I was quite excited. It allowed me to arrange a few days stopover to track Moses down and see for myself how Michelangelo had depicted this great Biblical figure. I had no trouble recognising Sarah's photo that fateful night.

'But back to the Bible scholars. It seems that to state that Jerome's rendering of the original Hebrew as *cornuta esset facies sua* was an error in interpretation and translation is too simplistic a statement, indeed it is incorrect.

'Scholars of ancient Hebrew agree that the original admits either translation: "his face was radiating light" or "his face was horned". The challenge confronting translators is to convey into the target language the intended ambiguity of the Hebrew Torah. This not really being possible, it remains for one of the two options to be selected.

'It is generally accepted that Jerome's "horn" was not a mistranslation but a deliberate choice. He was certainly aware of the possibility of using either of the two options. This is made clear in his own writing.' Here once again Colin referred to his notes and then continued, 'He writes in his commentary on the book of Ezekiel: *Finally after forty days the common people with their clouded eyes could not look at Moses' face because it had been "glorified" or as they say in the Hebrew "horned".*

'He chose "horned" here knowing that it was used on a number of occasions in the Old Testament but always in a metaphorical sense. Horns are seen as symbols of honour, strength and power. These qualities suited his vision of this leader. As you can imagine I was very excited to have seen Michelangelo's actual sculpture.

'This statue has given rise to a whole range of academic pursuits. Discussion on a suitable translation is only one of the aspects which has drawn the attention of scholars. Others revolve around the mood expressed, the tablets which Moses is holding, his posture, which incident in his life it might represent, its history; the list goes on.

'To this day Moses sits in his allotted place — the central focus of the tomb of Pope Julius II — challenging the visitors to understand him. So, if any of you are ever in Rome, search out the basilica of St Peter in Chains and spend some time admiring this work of beauty.

'Most English translations of the relevant text today do not favour the "horned" option. My RSV, for example, reads, and I have made a copy here: *When Moses came down from Mount Sinai, with the two tablets of the testimony in his hands as he came down from the mountain, Moses did not know that the skin on his face shone because he had been talking with God.* I'm sure Moses would have preferred to have a blushed face rather than have two horns growing out of his forehead. Ah, the paths our Holy Scripture will lead us down if taken too literally!'

It was clear to an observer that the attention of some of Colin's audience was starting to waver mid-way through his talk. Fingers were fidgeting, feet shuffling and eyes wandering. Andrew, although as a tertiary student he was used to sitting through lectures which could be wearying, found himself jumping awake as Colin had Moses coming down from the mountain.

His eyes also began moving around the room in an attempt to keep them open. They settled on Tony and noticed that his head was bent forward with eyes closed. He let his friend sleep. They then moved to Sarah, standing off to one side moving slowly from one leg to the other. His dreamy eyes stayed there, and his attention moved to there as well. He found it really difficult to follow what Colin was saying even though his eyes and mind were only a few metres from him. In reality they were directed elsewhere.

'But that's another story and I had better stop there,' concluded Colin. 'Thank you all very much for listening to me.'

There was a loud round of applause. Tony's head jerked up. Sarah moved to the front again and thanked Colin. 'Now we'll move out to the front of the church and meet at St Jerome's statue, and Colin,' she added, 'you can be my expert offsider any time you like.'

Colin blushed. Andrew kept looking at Sarah until she happened to look in his direction. He looked away quickly.

'Come on, Sleepyhead, it's time to get moving.' Tony interrupted his friend's train of thought.

'You can talk! I saw you sleeping half way through Colin's talk but was too polite to wake you up,' Andrew replied.

'Yes, he did go on a bit, but some seemed to be interested in what he had to say.'

'I was,' Andrew admitted. 'It is interesting how a statue in Rome, a different translation in the Vulgate, Michelangelo, Jerome and we all meet up here in Bethlehem in a cave.'

'Yes, I didn't realise that I would have to be a spelunker when I agreed to come to Israel with you.'

'A what?' asked Andrew, puzzled at what Tony was getting at.

'A spelunker. You know. An idiot who goes crawling around in caves. They've got to be batty.'

'Very funny!' But Andrew had to smile. 'So, let's do a little bit of spelunking ourselves and look at those other caves Sarah mentioned.'

After spending a short while looking at other caves in the complex they made their way out of the Church of St Catherine and joined a few others waiting near the statue of S. HIERONYMUS.

*Statue of St Jerome located in front of the Church of St Catherine in Bethlehem.*

## Chapter 7

# First Night Dinner

Andrew and Tony moved up to the last two seats at a dining table which was proudly displaying a small Australian flag. After their first full day on tour the faces already seated there were familiar, but they could not yet put names to all of them. They were welcomed with smiles and a 'Please join us'. As would be expected, the conversation soon turned to a discussion and assessment of the day's activities.

'Well, I'm absolutely buggered,' began Tony; but noting the frown on Pastor Paul's forehead he added by way of an apology, 'Oops, sorry, Pastor Paul and others. Change that to absolutely worn out.' Then turning to Margaret Schneider and her companion whom he had met briefly in the Shepherds' Field, he continued, 'How did you older ladies pull up?'

'I beg your pardon, younger man,' returned Margaret, as her friend, Avril Baumgartner, sat up a little straighter, 'we "pulled up" as you termed it, very well thank you. Indeed, Avril and I have had a most inspiring day. Haven't we Avril?'

'Yes, indeed,' took up Avril, as she attended to a few wayward wisps of hair which had detached themselves from the neat bun at the back of her head. 'I still find it hard to realise that I am here in the Holy Land walking in the footsteps of the Lord. I was so excited walking down from the Mount of Olives, thinking "Jesus walked here". Down to that little church. What was its name? It was Latin wasn't it?'

The Pastor's wife came to the rescue. 'That would be the Chapel of Dominus Flevit, Avril.'

'That's right, Dominic save it. That is where Jesus cried when he saw Jerusalem. Yes, and then there was the one down the bottom with the colourful front. I didn't catch why the United Nations built it. And I loved those old olive trees near the church. Someone said that they were alive when Jesus suffered in the Garden of Gethsemane there.'

'I was disappointed that we couldn't get to go inside the Dominus Flevit Chapel,' said Andrew, not picking up on Avril's reference to the age of the olive trees. He had bought a small point-and-shoot camera especially for the trip and was anxious to make good use of it. 'I had seen a photo taken from inside the building looking through a window to the Moslem Dome on the Rock and ....'

'Dome **of** the Rock,' corrected Colin, who had been listening but saying little.

'Whatever,' continued Andrew not taking any offence. 'I wanted to take a photo just like the one I saw on the net. That's always the way. You look forward to doing something and then when you finally get round to doing it you find that something gets in your way. I remember when I went to Adelaide...'

'I know what you mean,' butted in Colin. 'I was in Europe two years ago and everywhere I went things were either closed for renovations or covered over with scaffolding. I called it the great European Cover-up. I'll tell you what I mean. I went to see Mount Glockner but when I got there it was covered with fog. Even the fog gods were against me.'

'Where on earth is Mount Glockner?' someone wanted to know. 'And why did you want to see it?'

'Oh, I'm sorry,' continued Colin. 'Mount Glockner is the

highest mountain in Austria. I love mountain landscapes. I also like to know the name of the place or peak that I'm photographing.'

'That makes sense,' remarked Pastor Paul. 'I suppose it's a bit like taking photos of people. You want to know whether it's Uncle Vic, Aunty Mable, Joe Blow or whoever. Unless of course, if you were taking a photo for artistic purposes. Then it's the art in the photo and not so much the actual people that's important. The person is only a model...'

Margaret and Avril were less interested in discussing the finer points of art photography and were still back in the Garden of Gethsemane.

'You know what struck me while walking among those olive trees near that United Nations Church?' asked Margaret, directing her question to her friend.

'Was it the old gnarled trees?' suggested Avril.

'No, not exactly the look of the old trees themselves. It was how fresh, young shoots were growing out of the base of those ancient, stumpy trees. I've had something in my mind ever since and for some reason I've just remembered what it was.' Margaret stopped for a moment and thought.

'Well, what was it?' prompted Avril.

'It was that Old Testament Bible verse we had to learn for the Christmas program when I was a kid. Probably from Isaiah, but I don't really remember.'

'Well?'

'It went something like "a shoot will grow up from Jesse's stump and a branch growing out of his roots will bear fruit". Do you remember it?'

'Yes, that does ring a bell, but I don't remember ever learning it by heart. What about it?'

'Well,' said Margaret, 'don't you see how those old olive trees are telling us the same thing. That Old Testament verse makes much more sense to me now.'

'There's no doubt about you, Margaret. You see the Bible in everything.'

Tony had been half listening to these — to his way of thinking — rather prim old biddies and he asked, 'Did you take a photo of those old trees and their babies? That would make them easier to remember.'

'No,' replied Margaret, 'I didn't really come on this trip to take photos. I'm excited here when I see places and things around me that remind me of Bible texts and stories. Then later when I'm back home and reading my Bible I will often be reminded of what I saw and experienced here.'

Andrew was listening and joined in. 'I think that's a great way to get the most out of your pilgrimage here.'

'Why, thank you, young man,' said Avril. 'But I think it's getting time two old ladies like us were making our way up to bed.' And she smiled at Tony.

With that, she and her friend Margaret, got up, said their good-nights and made their way from the dining hall. Colin also excused himself and this left Pastor Paul and his wife sitting opposite Andrew and Tony.

Tony had been looking around the dining room and his eyes settled on a small table for four with only three people sitting at it. He assumed that the three were a family of parents and their daughter, who seemed to be eighteen or nineteen years old. He and Andrew had noticed them on the bus that morning, but they did not have the opportunity of meeting them during the day. Tony now saw his opportunity.

'Say, Pastor,' he began, 'do you know anything about those three people sitting across there by themselves? They are part of our group, aren't they?'

Pastor Paul looked across. 'Oh, yes. I was introduced to them last night but for the life of me I can't remember their names. I will have to consult my list and check up. Why do you ask?'

Andrew looked at Julie, raised his eyebrows and smiled. Julie got his meaning and smiled back.

In all seriousness Tony said to Pastor Paul, 'It seems a little rude to leave them sitting there by themselves. I might go over and have my dessert with them.'

'Fine,' agreed Pastor Paul. 'I believe they're from Adelaide and that is their daughter.'

With a 'see you later' to Andrew, Tony moved over to, as Andrew said to Julie, spread his charm around.

He had gone, and Paul turned to Andrew, 'You're not off to your room yet?'

'No, but it's been a pretty full-on day and I don't think it will be much longer before I will be heading up to my room ... or is it down to my room?'

'Gordon told me that you have had some health issues and I was hoping you might be happy to give me some idea of what you have been through. But only if you want to.'

'Sure, it's no big secret,' Andrew replied happily. 'It all began earlier this year. I noticed that I had a slightly sore throat a lot of the time. Then I started getting light headaches and found that I had trouble concentrating and I had no energy.'

'You were probably worried about your sore throat and headaches and that took your mind off things.'

'It seems as though that could have been the case,' replied Andrew. 'Eventually one of the lecturers at the Academy convinced me I had to see a doctor about it. That began a whole series of tests and procedures. It was quite a worrying time, not only for me but for my whole family and of course the people at the Academy.'

'I can imagine that. I'm sure you would have been in the prayers of many of your acquaintances.'

'Anyway, to cut a long story short, they eventually established that I had some sort of cancerous growth at the back of my tongue and had to undergo a program of chemo. That appears to have done a good job and the specialists are confident of a positive outcome. But they can't really be sure. I am sort of recuperating at the moment and will have to undergo scans when I return to Australia, to see if further action will be needed.'

'Julie and I really feel for you, Andrew. I hope and pray that all will have been cured and that you can get on preparing for your future vocation.'

'Amen to that, Pastor Paul. And thank you. But I am positive and try to continue as though everything is OK.'

'Good for you,' said Julie who had been very interested in Andrew's journey.

Then Pastor Paul continued, 'And I hope that your trip here will not only keep your mind off your medical problems and the doctors you left back in Australia but most importantly that you will feel the Lord's presence still here and draw strength and comfort from that. May he bless you and keep you well Andrew.'

Andrew was about to get up from the table when Gordon, the tour leader walked up. He had been going from table to table gauging how the day had gone and making sure there were no problems.

'Thank you for all you did today, Pastor Paul. You had a very good selection of songs on the song booklet which you produced for the trip. A few have mentioned to me how they appreciated it.'

'That's OK,' was Pastor Paul's modest reply and then he went on. 'Actually, Julie did most of the work compiling it and choosing the songs. She tried to make sure there was one relevant to each site we will be visiting.'

'That's great, but they probably won't all be needed. I don't envisage that we will be singing at every site we visit.'

'I can see that will be the case,' said Julie, 'but they are there just in case.'

'And Andrew, how has your day been? Not too much for you?'

'To tell you the truth, Gordon, I'm quite done in. It has been a very hectic day; but enjoyable. I'm tired, but it's nothing a good night's sleep won't fix.'

'I'm pleased about that,' replied Gordon. 'Be careful, for I didn't bring you all this way to make matters worse for you.'

'Don't worry,' Andrew assured him, 'I'll take things easy. I wouldn't want you and Tony to be carrying me around. Not that he would have the time. He seems too busy chatting other people up.'

Andrew looked at Julie who smiled back at him and they both looked across to the table where Tony was talking to the couple and their daughter.

'To tell you the truth, I'm very happy to see how members of this group seem to be getting on. I've had times when things have not gone so smoothly. But this time I'm already convinced that things will go very well. Like those two couples over there. Waller and Gersekowski are their names. Have you met them already? No? Anyway, they seem to be getting along very well together.'

'Yes, indeed,' noted Pastor Paul, who looked towards their table. 'They seem to have plenty to talk about.'

'It's interesting however,' Gordon continued, 'for it is not the two men who have hit it off so well. But Gary, that's Gary Waller, and Stephen's wife, Frances, are the ones who seem to have more in common. They appear to be more interested in the sites we have visited here and their Biblical connections. Their partners seem to have other interests.'

'It's great that you are so pleased about how everything is going, Gordon. Paul and I are very excited. We've had a great day and can't wait for things to continue.'

## Chapter 8

# Reprise

The tour bus was driving into the second day of pilgrimage experiences for the group from down under. A usual, Sarah had welcomed them all on board with a cheery *Boker Tov* and after everyone had settled into their chosen seats, she took the microphone. 'Before I outline what is exactly ahead of you today Tony Jackson has agreed to remind you of yesterday. Actually, I asked him last night if he could do this for me and he readily agreed.'

'Trying to get on your good side, no doubt, hey Sarah?' came from the back of the bus with an accompaniment of chuckles.

Sarah blushed slightly and then continued, 'Actually it was Margaret Schneider who dobbed him in. I don't know what he has been saying to her. That doesn't matter. Tony, would you come up to the mike, please?'

After a few brief, barking coughs to clear his throat Tony's clear tenor voice echoed through the bus. Those who had not really stopped talking to listen to Sarah were suddenly silent.

*'Jerusalem the Golden,*
*With milk and honey blessed;*
*I know not, oh, I know not*
*What joys await us here ...'*

Then he stopped singing. 'I was just trying to copy the voice of Harry Secombe on an old, scratchy piece of vinyl I have at home. Actually, it's my Dad's, not mine; long before my time!

For me, it was Secombe who accompanied the song on our bus's PA yesterday as we made our way along the Rabaa-al-adwaya to the Mount of Olives. I don't know, Sarah, but did we drive along the Rabaa-al-adwaya? No matter. It rolls off the tongue. Yes, we were going to see for ourselves what awaited us there. And we did see. The emotion of it all. What a moving beginning and a wonderful time of reflection on the Mount looking out over this ancient city, all with their own private thoughts. Then it all began moving more quickly.'

Tony extracted a sheet of paper from his pocket, took a deep breath and read as quickly as he could. 'That initial panoramic view, the oohs and aahs and the odd tear, the dome of the rock, watch out for pickpockets, the man and his donkey, beautiful view, only two dollar, the wall, which wall? the dome of the rock, the valleys, in the shadow of death, the green line, temple mount, palm sunday road with bitumen and taxis, the crowds were there but where were the palms? the chapel of dominus flevit, dominus who? franciscans, maroochy, pavarotti, antonio barluzzi, yes, barluzzi, we shall meet him again, teardrops from heaven, church of the nativity, white limestone buildings, windmills, chickens under my wings, graveyards, stones, you must build this way, hedron valley? no kidron, hell, ottoman empire, ossuaries, necropolises, the jerusalem cross, peter and his rooster, st pierre en gallicante, armenians and greeks, orthodox and roman catholics, dominicans and franciscans, the stump of jesse, olive trees which refuse to die, church of the nativity, o jerusalem! jerusalem! as the deer pants for the water, vulgate, st catherine, hadrian, 386ad or is it ce? no ce. 530ad, queen helena, why do you sleep, atms, cabramatta, parramatta, oodnadatta, what the hell, what's it all matter? 24th december, 2nd january, 19th january, united nations, united nations? no the church of the nations, doric, ionian or corinthian, byzantine, and the cock crowed thrice, in the shepherds' field, o little town of bethlehem, who's boaz? shopping, dancing with the turks, retail therapy, constantine and caiaphas, king solomon and the queen.'

Then Tony's voice took over with the words of a song he knew well from Lerner and Loewe's *Brigadoon*: '*What a day this has been, what a real whirl I'm in. Why it's almost like falling in love.*'

He stopped, looked at Sarah and smiled. Then he looked at the other tourists sitting in the bus and asked, 'What! Could you not keep up with me for one day?'

There were loud cheers and clapping throughout the bus. When this had died down Tony continued, 'And I must tell you that this has not been all my own idea and work. Andrew and I were up to all hours last night deciding what I should say.'

Tony moved back to his seat beside Andrew. Sarah took the microphone. 'What can I say? Thank you, Tony and Andrew. Especially you Tony. I didn't think you would need Andrew to help you decide to say something!' Then she slowly outlined the itinerary for the day.

Andrew looked at his friend and nodded. 'You did a great job. But why did you embarrass Sarah at the end like you did?'

'Embarrass Sarah? What do you mean?'

'The way you looked at her and smiled after singing about falling in love. We didn't plan that last night.'

'Don't worry. I'm sure she can take a joke.'

*A pilgrimage where the sites, images and experiences keep mounting.*

## Chapter 9

# Hezekiah's Tunnel

Gordon was seated in the front of the coach and took over the microphone when Sarah had finished outlining the day's activities. He gave a few positive remarks about Tony's summary of the previous day and hoped they hadn't found it too confusing. Then he said he wanted to prepare everyone for the first stop of the day and continued, 'Many years ago when I was just a small kid in primary school...'

'It was probably longer than many,' remarked someone sitting right next to him.

'Thank you, Jim, but you of all people should remember that I started getting grey hairs and wrinkles when I was still quite young. Now, as I was about to say. Our primary school teacher was keen to instil a love of poetry into his pupils. One method he used was to try and have us learn complete poems. I don't think any of us actually ended up learning a whole poem, so that method didn't really achieve his aim. Another approach he used was to analyse the rhythm of the language of the poem. Yes, sounds very academic; but not really. As a result of this approach, I can still recite parts of poems which have an iambic rhythm.'

'OK. Let's hear one,' suggested his old mate Jim.

'Iambic. That's the one that goes da-DAH da-DAH da-DAH and so on. Now let me think,' continued Gordon. 'Here's a good Australian one. *I love a sunburnt country, a land of sweeping plains, of ragged mountain ranges, of droughts and flooding rains.*'

At this stage there was loud applause and yahooing throughout the coach. Then Gordon sarcastically acknowledged his audience and called for silence.

'OK. OK. Thank you. Do you really know that poem?'

'Don't get him started,' warned Jim.

'Right, Jim, I didn't really want everyone to have to put up with one of my poetry presentations. What I really want to illustrate now is a rhythm called anapaest. Here two unstressed syllables are followed by one stressed syllable. It goes like this: da-da-DAH, da-da-DAH, da-da-DAH, da-da-DAH. This was our favourite for it could be seen as the rhythm of a galloping horse and being country kids, we all loved galloping horses. Then we had to learn poems of this type. I remember part of one. It is a poem by Walter Scott called *Young Lochinvar*.

> *O the young Lochinvar is come out of the west*
> *Through all the wide border his steed was the best;*
> *And save his good broadsword he weapons had none.*
> *He rode all unarmed and he rode all alone.*
> *So faithful in love, and so dauntless in war,*
> *There never was knight like the young Lochinvar.*

'Can't you feel the galloping steed which young Lochinvar is riding. All together now. Da-da-**DAH**, da-da-**DAH**.'

Soon everyone had joined in and the bus was galloping along through the streets of Jerusalem. When the exuberant da-da-DAHing was eventually reined in and quiet restored once more, Gordon continued, 'The story keeps going with this beat but I will leave you in suspense and not recite what happened. There was another I remember by the English poet Lord Byron called *The Destruction of Sennacherib*. This was based on the story of King Sennacherib of Assyria, attacking Judah, especially Jerusalem, in around 700 BCE. The biblical account is found somewhere in Kings, as I remember. I had looked it up but have forgotten exactly where. Lord Byron wrote:

*The Assyrian came down like the wolf on the fold,*
*and his cohorts were gleaming in purple and gold,*
*And the sheen of their spears was like stars on the sea,*
*When the blue wave rolls nightly on deep Galilee.*

The whole poem is written in the rhythm of the Assyrian cavalry.'

Some in the coach had even started da-da-DAHing and another was heard to say, 'Quiet, you two! Give him a go.'

Then Gordon continued, 'Who would have thought that many years after learning this poem by heart in school it would come to mind when I first visited a great engineering achievement in Jerusalem. Well, the first line came to mind and I had to look up the rest! I've learnt it especially for you. It talks about the time in history when our next site was constructed. It is a great example of ancient engineering. As Sarah has just told you, that's where we are now headed.'

That engineering marvel was Hezekiah's tunnel. This is a tunnel, 533 metres long, chipped through solid rock to bring water from a spring outside the walls of Jerusalem to the Pool of Siloam in the ancient City of David (Jerusalem). It was constructed 2700 years ago at that time described in Lord Byron's poem when Hezekiah was the King of Judah and he was being attacked by the Assyrian army lead by Sennacherib.

Many find it very interesting to read the stories about those early kings of Judah and Israel (the northern kingdom) and how the biblical writers gave them a pass mark or a failure. King Joash, for example, *did what was right in the eyes of the Lord* (2 Kings 12:2). He was given a tick. Johoash, however, *did evil in the eyes of the Lord* (2 Kings 13:11) and got a cross. Hezekiah, King of Judah from 715 BCE to 686 BCE, was one of the good guys, for he *did what was right in the eyes of the Lord* (2 Kings 18:3).

At this particular time in the history of Israel and Judah, it was not easy for a king to be a good guy. This whole area was caught up in the expansion of the powerful Assyrian Empire. The options available to the small kingdoms in the region were very limited. They could submit to the invading Assyrians and become a vassal state, pay huge tribute and accept the conditions placed on them. Amongst other things this involved accepting the gods which the victors brought with them. In this way they continued to exist.

On the other hand, they could resist, suffer inevitable defeat, and basically cease to exist as a nation. Israel chose to defy the Assyrians and this lead to their ultimate defeat in 722 BCE. Most of their citizens were deported and replaced by groups from other countries.

Judah initially escaped the calamity which befell her northern neighbour Israel. King Ahaz, their ruler at the time signed away his liberty and Judah became a vassal state. He had to pay huge taxes and gradually he allowed religious practices that were contrary to that demanded by the God of the Israelites. When he died — and he was not given a tick by the ancient writers — his son, Hezekiah, became ruler and he attempted to do what was right in the eyes of the Lord. He continued paying tribute but gradually began restoring worship of their true God.

He did this just as a new ruler, Sennacherib, had taken control in Assyria. Hezekiah perceived that Sennacherib was not as powerful as the previous ruler, Sargon II, and so took this gamble. He also realised that his actions would not go unnoticed and that the enemy would soon come with their demands. They did come, but Hezekiah was prepared. Jerusalem was heavily fortified by its walls and this would repel the attackers. However, it was open to siege warfare. The enemy would camp around the city and starve the inhabitants into submission.

His plan was to deny the attacking army a source of water while ensuring that the citizens within the city walls of Jerusalem would have sufficient supplies. Hence, he had the main water supply of the area diverted under his city to pools within the walls, unavailable to the attackers. And so, Hezekiah's tunnel was constructed to frustrate the siege by the Assyrians.

Today the tunnel is a great attraction for visitors to Jerusalem. They have the opportunity to *wade in the waters, wade in the waters children*, and walk the length of the tunnel. Knee-deep, cool water still runs the length of the tunnel. Walking along, one has to recognise the skill of the workers who did the digging.

It is remarkable that these men were able to achieve this result with the technology available at that time. We are told that there were two teams, one beginning at each end. How they knew that they would meet and not end up digging TWO tunnels remains a mystery. The final result does have an "S" shape so maybe they went off course at times. Or maybe it was meant to be S-shaped. And there are short dead-end arms along the way. Were they errors of direction or simply made for some specific purpose?

But how lovely it was for the visitors walking in the water through this man-made tunnel. Water was dripping from the walls and ceiling of the tunnel. This was limestone country which generally is noted for limestone caves with amazing formations created by deposits from the dripping water. Throughout the world there are many famous caves with stalactites and stalagmites and columns. These are natural creations which have taken millions of years to develop. Here in Hezekiah's tunnel the beginnings of stalactites, little projections 2-3 centimetres long hanging from the ceiling, could be discerned. They were building slowly but surely. Those visitors who come in a few thousand years time will see that they will be twice as long.

Gordon and his pilgrim group made their way slowly through this ancient tunnel. Torches flashed up, down and sideways lighting the way. The height particularly needed to be lit up for solid limestone yields little to the bumping of a human head.

Then the singing began. Clear voices echoed through the darkness. The acoustics were as good as in the showers back home. The songs gave expression to the joyful mood of the visitors, a musical word of praise to God and helped a few with threatening claustrophobia. It was appreciated by others in the tunnel as well. A group of Chinese girls who followed them expressed their thanks for the music. They thanked Andrew and Tony not knowing that their contribution to the choir was less than meagre. They should have thanked Pastor Paul and others whose voices made the limestone ring.

And did the tunnel help Hezekiah and save Jerusalem? The jury is still out. Sennacherib's army did lay siege to Jerusalem. For many months their nightly campfires could be seen flickering on the Mount of Olives and other surrounding hills, an ominous precursor of impending fate. But the city was not defeated. For some reason the Assyrian forces suddenly withdrew. The biblical writer (2 Kings 19:35-36) declares: *That night the angel of the Lord went out and put to death a hundred and eighty five thousand men in the Assyrian camp. When the people got up the next morning — there were all the dead bodies! So Sennacherib, king of Assyria, broke camp and withdrew. He returned to Nineveh and stayed there.*

Or in the words of Lord Byron keeping true to this biblical explanation (and keeping the beat of galloping horses — retreating this time):

*For the Angel of Death spread his wings on the blast,*
*and breathed in the face of the foe as he passed;*
*And the eyes of the sleepers waxed deadly and chill*
*And their hearts but once heaved and forever grew still!*

Other historians suggest other reasons for the Assyrian withdrawal in which God and his angel played no role. Jerusalem remained free; but for not much longer. In 587 BCE the Babylonians conquered the city and marched many of its citizens off into captivity. The tunnel remained.

The tunnel also prompted many of its visitors to look once again at some of those kings of ancient Israel — the good guys and the bad — the ticks and the crosses.

This walk back through time was an enjoyable experience for most, but some were quite relieved when they saw the daylight at the end of the tunnel. Gradually they came out from the darkness of ancient times into the twenty-first century and sat around what is thought to be the ancient Pool of Salom, describing their feelings to one another. They were assembled waiting for everyone to emerge from the eighth century BCE.

'Where's Emma?'

'She decided not to come. Said she was afraid of the dark and never did like swimming.'

'What about those two young fellows? Aren't they out yet?'

Gordon looked around. They were nowhere to be seen. 'Have they gone on ahead and not waited here?' he asked no one in particular.

But no one had seen them emerge from the tunnel. Margaret and Avril claimed to have seen them in the tunnel.

'They were in one of those short, dead-end passages,' said Margaret. 'Just standing there and splashing people as they came around the corner.'

'Yes,' agreed Avril. 'That's why my jacket is so wet. Margaret told them a thing or two, I can tell you!'

Sarah had been looking around as well making sure all had come out safely.

'Colin,' she said, 'Colin with the cameras. He's not here either. Surely he's still not in there taking photographs. Has anyone seen him?'

A number of heads shook in the negative. Sarah went up to Gordon and the two of them were preparing to go back into the tunnel when a cheer went up. They looked and saw the three men emerging arm in arm. But the cheer died down when it was realised that the three were not all arm in arm, but the two younger men on the outside were supporting, half carrying, Colin between them. They brought him out into the light and sat him down on a block of stone beside the pool. Soon many of the group were crowding around wanting to know what had happened.

Gordon and Sarah rushed over. 'Colin, what happened? Are you OK?' Gordon looked very concerned.

'I don't know,' replied Colin. 'All of a sudden I felt funny and dizzy in there.'

'Was it claustrophobia?'

'No, I've never been bothered by confined spaces. No, I think it was all of those steps we had to climb down at the beginning. I took them too quickly and the exertion caught up with me and I suffered as a consequence. Lucky these two young fellows were there to look after me. But I think they felt quite ashamed after splashing me first.'

'Do you need someone to check you out?' Sarah was also concerned.

'No. I'll sit down here for a while and should then be OK.'

'Well, if you really think so,' said Sarah. 'We'll see how you feel in a while. Make sure you are honest and tell us if you haven't recovered.' Then she turned to Tony and Andrew. 'Thank you, you two. I suppose we owe you one.'

'I'll keep that in mind,' cheekily replied Tony, raising his eyebrows.

Andrew looked at her and smiled but said nothing.

*A Tristram's starling on a rocky ledge at Masada.*

## Chapter 10

# Masada

MASADA, 73 CE:

He sat on a hard rock up there in what had been the safety of the Masada fort, surrounded by the laughter of children and the weeping of those who had shared his self-imposed exile. A blackbird sat on the dead branch of a shrub beside him. With bowed head and heavy heart, he sat and thought, 'Tonight I am going to die.' As the brave warrior he was, he did not think, 'Tomorrow I might be killed in battle,' or even, 'Tomorrow I might escape death in battle but be taken prisoner by the Romans and sooner or later die in chains.' No, for him there was no alternative. There was no tomorrow. All had been decided. He thought, 'Tonight I am going to die.'

'I have fought against the Romans, against those rulers who have oppressed my homeland and slaughtered my people. But I have lost my battle. I leave a land still ruled by foreigners. Is a self-inflicted death the reward for my efforts, for my worthless effort? Do I welcome death? Do I feel cheated? Was I born to die unrewarded? I ponder in doubt. Is my trust in my God so great, is my belief in an afterlife strong enough to overcome my utter disappointment, to combat my pressing doubt?

'Of one thing I have no doubt. Tonight, I die.'

Masada is remembered as the site where the last stand of the Jewish rebellion against the Roman occupation took place in 70

CE. After years of very unsettled times — and rebellion was in the air at the time of Jesus half a century earlier — things finally came to a head. Enraged by the actions of the Roman procurators, Pontius Pilate being the best known of these, and stirred on by the Zealots, all-out war between the Jews and the Romans erupted in 66 CE. The uprising was finally crushed by Titus in 70 CE when he broke Jerusalem's defence, completely destroyed the temple and razed the city.

The city was destroyed, the land conquered, but there was still a number of strongholds in the rebels' hands. The three main areas of resistance were Herodium, Machaerus and Masada. Herodium was a fort which Herod the Great had built on the summit of a man-made, circular hill 12 kilometres south of Jerusalem. Machaerus was a fortress east of the Dead Sea — now in the country of Jordan — in which it is thought John the Baptist was imprisoned and executed. These two were quickly conquered without a great deal of effort on the part of the Romans and also without great loss of life. Masada remained defiant.

Masada was in the Judean Desert, 50 kilometres south of Jerusalem overlooking the Dead Sea. Again, it was Herod who had a fort and luxurious palace built on the top of this steep-sided mesa when he was in power. It was built as a refuge for himself and his family. The cliff-like sides of the mesa rose very abruptly on all sides to a height of 400 metres. A successful attack up these slopes would not be easily achieved.

Already in 66 CE at the outbreak of hostilities, a fanatical Galilean zealot, Eleazar, and a group of his followers occupied this fort. From here he had been able to make raids against the Romans in the surrounding areas and then retreat to relative safely. Now with Judea conquered, he and his band stood alone against the might of the Roman forces. The victors would not allow his resistance to continue.

## Chapter 10   Masada

Thus began a long period of siege warfare for the Romans to overcome this remaining nuisance.

Over a period of many months the site was completely surrounded by a *circumvallatio*, a wall which ensured that those on the mesa top could not escape. Then a massive rampart was built, rock by rock, higher and higher, to gain close access to the walls of the fort — at least in one place. This allowed the Romans to bring their siege machines up to the wall which was soon breached. The defenders had built a second wall inside the outer one, and this hindered the progress of the attackers for some time. After it had been set alight and was crumbling, the Zealots knew that the next day would see the Roman soldiers begin their slaughtering.

Realising their hopeless position and knowing the fate of the women and children who were also living there, the decision was made that everyone would commit suicide and deny the attackers the taste of blood.

Next morning the Romans found only dead bodies and a burnt-out palace; a hollow victory. Thus, the spring of 73 CE saw the end of this Jewish uprising against the Romans.

This is a cruel tale, a barbaric tale, a tale of pride and determination against overwhelming odds. This heroic episode of previous times is one that has been printed indelibly in the annals of the Jewish people. It is similar to others, in different countries, which are found on the pages of history; fights which cannot be won. It is the gallant defeat which is remembered. Remember the Alamo, or the landing at Gallipoli?

Unlike the Roman soldiers of 1945 years ago who were struggling up a rampart, probably being targets for rocks being hurled down from above, Andrew and all the other members of his tour group sat in a cable car to arrive at the top of the Masada mesa. Andrew — and this was publically announced by his friend Tony

— could have walked up a zigzag path, steep and hot, but he wisely chose not to. Conserving energy, that's what Tony called it. It also gave him more time and opportunity to see and remember what was waiting for him at the top.

And what did he see?

He saw a number of blackbirds up there. Fairly friendly fellows they were too. The one he clearly remembered, as he explained to his dinner companions that evening, was looking less than happy, and seemed to be giving him a mouthful. He was, Andrew suspected, merely complaining about the heat, lack of food and water and his usually quiet home being overrun by tourists levelling phones at him, or in his case a Canon, a point-and-shoot variety.

This blackbird was actually a Tristram's starling. They are noted for their black, black appearance with bright orange feathers at the bottom of their wings. These feathers stand out quite remarkably when the bird is in flight, but sitting here on a rock this young fellow seemed to be bashfully hiding his colours. If one were to look carefully, as Andrew did, they could be discerned readily enough.

'Why the name, <u>Tristram's</u> starling?' could be asked. Henry Tristram was an English clergyman living in the nineteenth century who seemed to have spent an inordinate amount of time travelling overseas. One wonders how his parishioners took to this! His travels also took him to the Holy Land and in 1868 he published a book, *Natural History of the Bible*. This naturally was about Palestine and surrounding areas. A few years later (16 to be exact) he released another of his works, descriptively named *Fauna and Flora of Palestine*.

Besides being a clergyman, a traveller and author he was also an ornithologist. It was probably because of this string to his bow that this bird, seen by Andrew here on top of Masada, was named in honour of him. No doubt it had a local name before bearing Tristram's name but what it was, Andrew never did discover.

Now, the good Reverend Tristram being an ornithologist was probably enthralled to spend many hours observing the habits of these Masada blackbirds, but after a few friendly words, hearty thanks for posing for the photograph (actually Andrew took more than one) this twenty-first century visitor was happy to bid him farewell and look further.

Standing on the edge of the plateau, Andrew did look further, a good deal further. He looked into the distance where he saw the blue waters of the Dead Sea. This view was quite scenic, but it did not hold his attention for long. What really caught his eye was something much closer, down at the base of the plateau. Located there was the stone wall outline of one of the Roman legion's encampment areas. It was remarkable that after two millennia the stones were still there, not removed from where the soldiers, or their slaves, had placed them during the year-long siege which had taken place here.

In a way this answered a question for Andrew which had often popped up when reading about a city which had undergone siege warfare in its history. The question is this: What do soldiers do during their long hours of boredom, during these long days, and months, sitting and waiting for the opposition to starve into submission? This question probably arose out of a statement which he heard in various forms, each with the same meaning. War is something described as long periods (90%, 99%) of boredom punctuated by moments of excitement (sheer terror).

So, what do soldiers do when laying siege to a city? It became clear to Andrew what the Roman soldiers did. They built stone walls. Here in the Judean Desert stones were plentiful, so they built stone walls.

Sarah disturbed his quiet thinking. 'Enough daydreaming, let's move on. It is time now for us to climb down to see the lower level of Herod's palace. This was where he had his private, luxurious rooms.'

'Sounds good. Let's see how the other half lived 2000 years ago.'

'Other half? Decadent rulers, perhaps.'

'Point taken, but what did you mean by climb down?' asked Andrew.

Sarah explained. 'Yes, it's on a ledge way below the main level of the top of the plateau.'

'And?'

'We will need to walk down some steps.'

'So we don't have to climb, just walk down some steps?'

'How many steps exactly?' Tony, who had quietly sauntered up, entered the conversation.

'I don't really know. For some it might be more than for others. It probably depends on your state of fitness.' Then she added as an afterthought, 'For you two fit young men, great footballers so you've told me, it would probably be hardly any.'

Half of the group chose to go. They were most likely "the others" who thought their fitness was up to it. Without any dramas, merely some tired legs, they arrived comfortably at Herod's private chambers. The views were spectacular. The remaining structure there really did give signs of its previous beauty. All agreed that it was well worth visiting and a half-group photo was shot as evidence of their successful descent.

'Now we need to walk back up.' Sarah caused some closed, resting eyes to reawaken.

'How many steps were there? Did anyone count them as we were coming down?' someone wanted to know.

A number of mumbled "Nos", and a few shaking of heads was the reply.

'Jim, you and I will count them on the way back. Now no stopping or we might forget where we are up to. See if we arrive at the same number.' Andrew put the challenge to another older, but fitter-looking member of the party.

Agreed, and at the top they compared tallies. 168 was Jim's total and Andrew had 169. Then Tony commented, 'He always exaggerates his athletic prowess.'

Now back at the top it was time for everyone to cool off in the caldarium after the 168/9 steps climb. The sun beat down severely on the barren, rocky surface of the mesa and so they were all looking for a shady spot. There was shade in the partly restored caldarium. In its original operating mode, it was a hot room, probably for Herod's privileged guests. Those times had long passed. Tony was amazed at the level of technology evident in these ancient ruins from Roman times. In this room he could clearly see how it operated. He was impressed with the technology, sure, but not with the concept, even though some fanatics point to the health benefits of being over-heated.

He had never been a fan of being overly hot and enjoying excessively humid weather. He preferred sitting in his study with the AC set at 25 degrees, when outside it was a humid 40. Why create discomfort?

The tour around the plateau continued. There was so much of interest on top of Masada: an old synagogue, a Christian church, columbarium, bathing pool, large rock cisterns, store rooms, remnants of wall decorations, rock walls (can't get away from these in Israel), the enormity of Herod's whole project. So much to see.

After spending hours walking around mostly under a hot sun, in and out of store rooms, up and down steps, everyone was pleased to have a return ticket for the cable car. In the waiting-room of the cable-car station Tony called for the attention of those waiting. Sarah looked suspiciously in his direction wondering what was coming. Everyone looked at him.

'*To be or not to be?*' he began. '*That is the question—*
*Whether 'tis nobler in the mind to suffer*
*The slings and arrows of outrageous fortune,*
*Or to take up arms against a sea of troubles*
*And, by opposing, end them? To die, to sleep.*'

Here he stopped and smiled, then continued, 'Sorry everyone. I had to learn that in high school when we were studying Shakespeare's *Hamlet*. This is the first time that I've ever had the opportunity of using it.'

A number in the group looked at one another questioningly, wondering perhaps: 'Why was this an appropriate opportunity?'

## Chapter 11

# Dead Sea

From the lookout point on the top of the Masada Mesa the Dead Sea could be seen glistening in the east. It was beckoning the travellers down to experience something different. The call was heeded, and the cable car soon had them all off the mountain. The gift shop at the foot of the descent was also preparing the visitors for their visit to the Salt Sea. Here, pillars of salt, bottles of water, intriguing photographs and bags of mud vied for attention. For most of the touring party however, these offerings served to heighten their expectation rather than lighten their wallets.

The trip to their selected Dead Sea resort was short but did allow time for Gordon to introduce Colin who had agreed to present a brief musical item.

'This should put you all in the right mood,' said Gordon in his introduction. 'But I'll leave Colin to explain.'

'Do you remember...' Colin began and then stopped. 'On second thought, I should say, have you ever heard of Flanders and Swan?'

There were a few tentative nods but mostly his question was met with blank, puzzled faces.

'A brewery perhaps?' someone asked.

Colin shook his head and continued, 'Probably a bit before your time. Anyway, they were a popular English duo who entertained numerous Revue Theatre goers in the 50s and 60s. Yes, as I said, well before your time. They would present clever, amusing songs which they had composed themselves. This is the chorus of one I remember called *The Hippopotamus Song.*'

Then Colin's strong singing voice sounded through the PA system:

'Mud, mud, glorious mud
Nothing quite like it for cooling the blood.
So follow me, follow, down to the hollow,
And there let us wallow in glorious mud.'

When the clapping and cheering had died down Gordon took the microphone back. 'No prizes for guessing why Colin suggested that song to me. And I did know it; but to put things into perspective. It was my mother who had one of their records. Sarah?'

Sarah took the mike for her announcement. 'A couple of things. First, I would like us all to meet on the seats under the date palms when we get off the bus. You will see where I mean. As you know we have been reading a relevant section from the Bible at the various pilgrimage sites. The Dead Sea is more of a general interest spot rather than a place of religious significance. I have asked Phillip, who is a geography teacher, to tell us a little about it. And one thing more before you get too excited. We will be giving each of you a small plastic bag of mud.'

'A bag of mud? What on earth for?' Margaret Schneider wanted to know.

'I'm sorry. Didn't you know about it? That's what Colin was singing about. It is special Dead Sea mud to rub all over yourself. It's great for your skin.'

At this stage she was drowned out by loud moans. When these had subsided she continued, 'And we expect all of you to use them. It's a real experience.'

## Chapter 11  Dead Sea

'It's an experience I certainly will not be tasting,' commented Avril.

Tony was quick on the uptake. 'You don't have to taste it, Avril. You just need to rub it all over yourself. Like this.'

At this stage Tony stood up and, moving more like a pole dancer in a night club, pretended to apply the mud.

'Thank you, Tony,' Sarah interrupted the performance and the laughter. 'We've found in the past that it's a good idea to have a friend help you apply it evenly, especially on your back. And,' looking at Tony who she realised was about to say something, 'I'm sure Andrew would be happy to help you. But make sure you keep your mouth closed so you don't taste the experience. But seriously, folks, it's a great experience and I hope all of you will ... should I say "taste" it?'

It wasn't long before the bus had parked and the group moved to the seats as Sarah had asked them to do. After waiting a while for everyone to be present, for the restrooms had a strong appeal for some, Phillip had the attention of the group.

He began. 'As a geography teacher, and I do enjoy teaching this subject, I'm so excited to be here. I'm standing in a rift valley and am seeing what one really looks like. I would teach my students about them using photos and sketches, and I can tell you this; a diagram makes them less complicated than they are in reality. I can also imagine that many of you just want to be here and see whether you can really float on the water and read a book as you have seen on the tele. So rather than have me rave on, I suggest that if any of you have a question, related to the geography generally, you ask it and I shall attempt to give you an answer.'

There was agreement to this suggestion for immediately the first question was heard. 'Phillip, I noticed the sea level marker beside the road as we drove down from Jerusalem, but I haven't seen any others. How far below sea level are we here?'

'No, I haven't either, but I believe that where we are standing is about 420 metres below sea level. This makes it the lowest point on the earth's land surface. We are about as low as we can go. It's hard to realise, isn't it? Just standing here looking around, you would have no idea that we are so low. Oh, and they say that this highway on which we have been travelling is the world's lowest road.'

'And what about the water, Phillip? How deep is it? It looks as though it is quite shallow.'

'Don't be fooled by looks. I suppose that can apply to a lot of things. But to be serious, it is surprisingly deep. Around 400 metres.'

'We all know that it is very salty. Is this because it lies so far below sea level?'

'Not really. Inland lakes and seas only become salty when they have no water draining out of them. They lose their water only by evaporation and the salts which are brought by the streams flowing into them remain. Over time this builds up.'

'What about the Sea of Galilee? Is it salty too?'

'You will find out when we go there in a few days that the water there is fresh.'

'But isn't it below sea level too?'

'Yes, indeed. It is about 200 metres below sea level. But this is the point. Water flows in from the north and flows out the southern end. That's the Jordan River. This keeps it free of excessive amounts of salts.'

'I'm one of those looking forward to floating on the water. But will I be able to? I'm not as slim as I used to be.'

'You will have no worries. The sea has a 33% salinity level and it is this high amount of salt that makes it possible for anyone to float. They even say that when you are lying on your back it is difficult to put your feet on the bottom and stand up. The water wants to keep your legs floating. That's something that you can find out for yourselves.'

The questions kept coming until Sarah had to step in. 'This has been great. Thank you for all your questions and thank you, Phillip, for being our teacher. But we really have to stop it here. The water awaits us all; and the mud. I will be keeping my eyes open for any clean skins. The changing rooms are through there. And have fun.'

After a couple of hours, the floating experience was behind them and now with the mud all washed off there was time to relax with feet planted firmly on dry land. Time also to talk over afternoon tea, or beer, perhaps a glass of freshly squeezed pomegranate juice or maybe just a glass of clean, cool, fresh water.

'That was you behind the mud screen, wasn't it Avril?' Tony cheekily wanted to know.

'Yes. Margaret convinced me that I should get the feel of mud. I don't know what good it did me.'

'But,' continued Tony, 'it felt so slithery and slimy, so smooth and sensuous, that it had to be good for you.'

'It certainly was slippery,' commented Pastor Paul.

'Yes,' said Andrew. 'I was very surprised at its feel and I am no stranger to mud. As a child I was constantly exposed to it; playing in it, eating it, creating with it, throwing it, trampling through it, you name it. But this was a new experience.'

'Tell us more,' encouraged Sarah. 'You, muddy? And I had taken you to be a good, clean-living person.'

Andrew smiled at her and then began, 'Well, there was our local creek. It doubled as our swimming pool. The main swimming hole, just down from Steinhardt's place was wide, long and deep. Well to us kids it was. The water was fresh, clear and clean. The banks were made of rich, fertile black loam. This was good for growing crops and also for ... wait a minute, I'm getting ahead of myself.'

'I can see where the mud will be coming from,' put in Colin.

'Spot on,' continued Andrew. 'As a hot Saturday afternoon wore on, the banks became wetter and wetter, slippier and slippier and muddier and muddier. Teams were chosen and then mud fights would begin. The clear, clean home of the resident Jew fish and eels soon became a muddy water hole being totally abused by a group of shouting, shiny, muddy kids.'

Pastor Paul joined in the conversation. 'I can certainly see the fun in that. It is definitely better than sitting inside in front of a screen. But was that as healthy as our Dead Sea mud?'

'I don't know about the salts but it certainly was accompanied by plenty of physical exercise. Dodging mud balls, climbing up slippery banks, swimming backwards and forwards across the creek. This would have made it healthy'

'Yes, I suppose mud is mud,' said Julie.

Sarah jumped quickly to defend her homeland and the mud from the Dead Sea. 'We have very special mud here with a high concentration of salts and minerals. I believe there are over thirty different active ingredients and they give great results.'

'What for instance, Sarah?' Tony wanted to know.

'It can prevent hair loss,' began Sarah.

There was a splattering of laughter around the table for it was evident that Tony's hair was thinning on the back of his head.

'And,' she continued, 'it can reduce arthritic knee pain not only in older people but especially in young footballers.' She smiled.

'And that's not all. It can improve the appearance of facial skin and work to control the appearance of cellulite.'

At the mention of cellulite Andrew saw Tony's head move around and a wicked smile appeared on his face. He sensed that some comment, probably embarrassing and inappropriate, was about to be aired so he quickly interrupted, 'Our mud down on the creek bank also had great impact. The small stones, grit and rotting vegetation added an extra dimension to its feel.'

'Would grow better crops too,' suggested Colin.

'Right,' said Andrew and continued. 'It made better, firmer balls to throw. At the end of the day we often went home with bruises and scratches and sore eyes.'

'It was a great experience today,' concluded Colin. 'Thank Goodness we haven't ended up with a lot of scratches and sore eyes. I did however end up with some great photos of shiny white teeth and good healthy Dead Sea fun. And Sarah, just to let you know that Margaret and Avril wanted me to take some photos of them covered in mud to show you and the two boys here that they didn't chicken out. Right ladies?'

Everyone was suddenly distracted by loud voices coming from a table a short distance away. All heads turned in this direction.

'Sounds like someone is not happy?'

'Wait a minute,' said Colin, 'those two couples are from our party, aren't they Gordon?'

'Yes, they are. That's Gary Waller and his wife with Stephen and Frances Gersekowski. I wonder what's up? I've only recently remarked how well those two couples have been getting on.'

Gordon was about to make his way over to them but the voices had returned to normal. He decided that it would be better to wait and speak quietly to them at some later occasion. He knew from experience that it was generally better to allow folks to work through their own problems.

'Ever had a good blow-up on any of your tours?' Tony wanted to know.

'You know, Tony, whenever there is a group living closely together for a couple of weeks or more, there is always a chance of some disagreement. But also, I might add, for a little bit of romance too.'

'So, what's your betting for either of these on this trip?' Colin asked.

'It's a bit early to say, Colin. Do you have anyone in mind?'

Colin seemed embarrassed. 'No. It was merely a general question.'

\* \* \*

### Extract from Andrew's travel diary:

I could call you Red Seduction.

No, you are no fair maiden, secretively bathing, surrounded only by the evening air. You are standing boldly, your arm outstretched, ready to deliver your delights.

The moment I first saw you I was seduced. I had to have you. I had to taste the sweet nectar you had to offer. The royal blood red of your seduction. You Jezebel, you! Can I taste you now?

But alas, no. The marching flag at the head of our small group would not wait, would not stand still. That which is up ahead is awaiting us. It kept moving forward, striving towards the next, leaving me no time to tarry and taste.

But you would not go away. Should I be in the Shepherds' Field; you were there. You came with me to Bethlehem to remember the Saviour's birth. Should I climb the walls of the Holy City; you were there. In every alley, Arab, Jew, Christian, your arm was there beckoning, welcoming me. Even in the coolness of the Garden Tomb, your agent was there, on a tree, smiling, tempting.

For how long, oh, for how long shall we be apart?

You hid in the walls of God's own synagogue, even in the city where Jesus walked, talked and taught. There in the ruins of the Capernaum holy place you lay, rejected, but reaching. I smiled, walked away, waiting for another time, another place.

And I am weak. I could not refuse you. Here on the shores of the Dead Sea, I tasted of your sweetness, of your coolness. Here beside the Dead Sea, you brought life back into my tiring, salty, thirsting body.

Here beside the Dead Sea I had finally tasted your delights and was satisfied.

I must add that while I was reading through parts of this aloud, Tony called out from the bathroom, 'Are you writing about Sarah?'

'No, Big Ears, I am not. Just writing about having a glass of freshly pressed pomegranate juice!'

*Salt in the Dead Sea.*

Chapter 12

# Remembering Easter

The tour had started off at a very hectic pace and Gordon and Sarah were experienced enough to notice that some of the tour members were now showing less enthusiasm than on the first couple of days. They decided to change the itinerary slightly to have a much less strenuous day. There would be far less travelling in the coach, fewer sites to visit and walking would be kept to a minimum. The day would be divided by a more casual, less rushed lunch at a rooftop restaurant in the centre of old Jerusalem. All going to plan, everyone would be back at the hotel with plenty of time to relax before dinner.

Gordon presented the revised plans for the next day in a very positive manner. He spoke to the group after dinner. 'Sarah and I have noticed that some of you have been looking a little tired and so we have come up with a suggestion for tomorrow. This will involve a slight change in the set-down plans. We hope the day will be a little less rushed and not so tiring. It will give you a lot of interesting memories to take back home. Pastor Paul, would you like to fill in the details?'

'Yes, friends, tomorrow should be the highlight of our pilgrim journey here to the Holy Land. Easter, as you all know, is the main festival of our church year and tomorrow we will focus solely on this. We will bring together some of the main elements of our Holy Week. We will begin by visiting the Cenacle.' Here he paused for effect but noticed several people looking at one another with a puzzled look on their faces. He quickly realised what this meant and anticipated the question which would surely follow.

'Oh, I'm sorry. Some of you may not be familiar with the term Cenacle. It's another word for the Room of the Last Supper. It comes from a Latin word meaning dining room. Then we will walk along part of the Via Dolorosa and stop at a number of Stations of the Cross. This will take us to the Church of the Holy Sepulchre, probably the most sacred Christian pilgrim site. Finally, we will spend time in the peaceful surrounds of the Garden Tomb where we will celebrate Holy Communion as a whole group.'

Gordon then took over again, 'It might seem a lot, but you will see that it will not really be a long day. Oh, Pastor Paul, it's not like you to forget lunch. Yes, after our visit to the Church of the Holy Sepulchre we will be going to a very special restaurant where we have booked tables on the rooftop. You will have some great views over old Jerusalem from up there. Sarah, do want to add anything?'

'Not really, except to say that we will be going to one of my favourite restaurants in Jerusalem. I know the owner personally and he always looks after my groups very well. Perhaps someone has a question about tomorrow?'

Colin stood up. 'It's probably more a personal question but it has some reference to tomorrow. It's this, Sarah. I understand that you are a Jew and not a Christian. How do you feel when you take Christians to their very holy sites and see the emotional reaction which many of them must show?'

'I see what you are getting at, Colin. Yes, I do follow the Jewish religion, but I don't see a conflict between that and my job as a tour guide. Tomorrow, we are going to visit sites which I know are very important to Christians. My job is to see that you experience these places as fully as possible. I am able to explain their history and the traditions related to them. All this is mainly factual, and I can do all this without becoming emotionally involved.'

'Thank you for that. I understand what you are saying,' said Colin, 'but don't you sometimes feel a little uncomfortable knowing that your faith rejects what the Christians might believe concerning some places?'

'No, not really,' Sarah was ready with the reply. 'My job is not to judge the faith of others. I don't only take Christian groups but also others as well: Moslem, Chinese, non-religious, you name them. I explain the sites as I understand them and answer their questions as best I can. My personal beliefs are not relevant in any of these situations.'

Gordon butted in at this point. 'That was a very interesting question, Colin. I hope you understand that Sarah is a great guide with great contacts and a wealth of information about tourist sites in Israel. We are visiting mostly Christian sites but don't forget Israel has many other tourist attractions which have little or nothing to do with Christianity.'

'Yes,' said Colin, 'I realise that. I also want to say that I think Sarah has been doing a wonderful job.'

With that there was applause and a few appreciative shouts. When this had died down, Gordon suggested that other questions could wait until tomorrow and wished everyone good night.

\* \* \*

'Well, that was indeed a day to remember,' Avril said to Phillip and his wife, Kaye, as they were sitting in the hotel lounge the next day after coming back from their Easter experience. 'That's what Gordon said last night, didn't he? I hoped that this would be the highlight of our trip.'

Phillip could sense that Avril wasn't really happy with the way the day had panned out. He hoped he wouldn't regret asking her why she seemed disappointed with the day's activities. 'So, what was the problem today, Avril?' he asked.

'Today? It started last night already when Gordon started talking about the cygnet, or whatever...'

Margaret interrupted, 'I think you mean the Cenacle, Avril, don't you?'

'Well yes, the Cenacle,' Avril continued. 'I knew then that we would be in for some problems. I had never heard of the word before. Why couldn't he just have said the Room of the Last Super, and left it at that, I don't know?'

'But everything seemed to go OK today, didn't it?' Kaye was interested to know why Avril didn't feel happy. 'I know I found the day very inspiring. What did you find so disappointing?'

'For a start, what did you think about the Room of the Last Supper or better still, the Upper Room? That's what I've always called it,' began Avril quite aggressively.

'Actually, I found the place very interesting; especially the architecture. The trouble was the room was a little crowded, but you could still see everything.' Phillip tried to be positive.

'The architecture? The only thing I remember is that someone was talking about that Moslem thing in the side wall. Do you remember what it was called? I don't.'

Phillip looked at his wife with a puzzled look on his face. 'Do you remember what it was called, Kaye?'

Kaye smiled and replied, 'It is a Mihrab. That indicates the direction a Moslem needs to face when praying. It shows the direction of Mecca from here.'

'That's what I mean,' Avril continued. 'Sarah was talking about its history and how it had been a mosque for many hundreds of years and stuff like that. There was nothing about the

## Chapter 12  Remembering Easter

Last Supper, Jesus washing the disciples' feet or Jesus appearing to his frightened disciples after he was crucified. We came here to see Christian things, didn't we Margaret?'

Margaret didn't respond to her friend's prompting. Phillip was thinking desperately of something to say which might assuage her when luckily Tony and Andrew appeared, each carrying a bottle of beer.

'Hello,' said Tony cheerfully, 'relaxing after our long day? Or should I say our less strenuous day?'

They put their bottles down on the table, commandeered a couple of vacant nearby chairs and joined the four who were already sitting there.

'So how did you two young fellows find today?' asked Phillip. He was always interested in the wide range of attitudes one finds in any group of people. He was finding this travelling group particularly intriguing. Here was a group, the majority of whom were worshipping members of the Lutheran Church of Australia, and already he had noticed widely differing reactions to what they were seeing. He was even taken aback on a few occasions at the opinions expressed by the pastor.

It all reminded him of a little exercise he would always give to a class when talking about vegetation. He would ask everyone to think about a tree, then write a description of it and also perhaps make a quick sketch of it. The class would always come up with a wide variety of responses. It wasn't because of their limited artistic or verbal ability. It was clear that each student had an individual idea of "tree". He would love to be able to ask this group to give him a statement of what they understand about God or Jesus. It was becoming clear how each member of this pilgrim group had his or her individual way of relating the Bible, the pilgrim sites and their faith.

Tony gave his impressions. 'I enjoyed the lunch. Had a few

local beers there which tasted quite OK. As for the Stations of the Cross and the Church of the Holy Sepulchre? I don't like saying this, but I wasn't at all impressed.'

'Oh,' remarked Phillip's wife, Kaye. 'So, what was the problem?'

'Well, all I could see along the Via Dolorosa were the stalls selling mementos and religious stuff. And in the Church of the Holy Sepulchre, the noise, the crush of people and the scaffolding where they were doing renovations just spoilt the whole atmosphere.'

'And what about you, Andrew?' Phillip wanted to know.

'Yes, I kind of agree with Tony about those places. For me the Garden Tomb was the real highlight.'

'I think I can tell you why, too,' began Tony as he looked at his friend.

They all looked towards Tony waiting for him to continue. Finally, he did. 'Well, he spent half the time sitting under a pomegranate tree talking to Sarah.'

Andrew felt a little uncomfortable but responded. 'Rubbish! It was only for a little while Tony. Certainly not half the time! Even after the short day I wasn't feeling too well and sat down in the shade there to rest for a while. Sarah must have seen that I was tired, and she came and joined me. Everyone else was happily looking around the gardens. She was happy to sit down and rest for a while as well.'

'Yes, the poor dear,' sympathised Margaret. 'She is always running about seeing to everyone. She is doing a great job and deserves to be able to sit down and rest now and then. But to get back to your comment, Andrew. Why was the Garden Tomb the highlight for you?'

'I found it so peaceful and restful after the noise and pushing of the other places we visited. To me, it represented what Easter means.'

## Chapter 12    Remembering Easter

'What do you mean?' Avril wanted to know. 'Easter is about the death and resurrection of our Lord. What more can there be?'

'I think different people see Easter in different ways, Avril. I'm sure many see it exactly as you do, but not everyone. You ask how it represented Easter to me. Let me explain. When I saw that empty tomb on display there in that garden setting I did not picture a dead person coming back to life. I thought that although the authorities, the Romans, had Jesus executed, it wasn't the end. The work he had begun did not stop but has continued and it still guides our lives today. The flowers, the lush grass and the green trees all create an atmosphere of peace and joy which is a sign of Jesus' presence. Jesus still lives.'

'I don't quite understand you, Andrew. Are you saying Jesus didn't rise from the dead?' Margaret asked this question.

'What I am saying,' explained Andrew, 'is that Jesus is alive here today and governs our lives. For us he is the Lord. All those other things in our lives that vie for our attention and that can influence us — our friends, family, the government and their strange laws, you name it — are not as important as Jesus.'

Phillip and Kaye were listening to this discussion without interrupting, but then Phillip did come forward with a question to Andrew. 'What about in the creed when we say Jesus was crucified, dead and buried and on the third day rose again. How do you see that?'

'To tell you the truth, I'm not real keen about creeds written centuries ago, in a different place, for different people, addressing different issues. And we repeat them parrot-fashion in our churches every Sunday. I'd rather see my life with Jesus as a creed.'

The others were noticing that Andrew was becoming somewhat restless. He was giving the impression that he didn't want to discuss this topic of Easter any longer. Did he feel that he was tying himself in knots or was he simply tired? This surprised them a little for he was always eager to discuss religious topics to the bitter end. They noticed that his eyes began surveying the lounge area. Rather than furthering the discussion, he stood up, excused himself and moved off.

Tony watched him as he made his way to the bar where Sarah was now standing. She smiled as he approached. After a few words, they moved off together, heading towards the hotel's main entrance.

Phillip was watching this as well. He turned to Tony and commented, 'I wonder what that's all about? And I wonder what they were really talking about under that pomegranate tree in the Garden Tomb?'

Chapter 13

# Sunday Worship

Sonntag, der neunte Oktober, und alle sind sehr früh aufgestanden, weil sie... Moment mal ...

Just a minute. They are going to the English church service at nine o'clock and not the German one. That changes everything. Let's start this all again!

It was Sunday, the ninth of October and everyone had risen early because they were going to a church service in the Holy City of Jerusalem.

The selected church, *Die Erlöserkirche* in Jerusalem must now be referred to as the Church of the Redeemer in Jerusalem. Different language, same church. This should be a memorable occasion for all concerned. Going to worship in this massive Lutheran Church in the middle of old Jerusalem was something special in the itinerary. And it is just a stone's throw from the Church of the Holy Sepulchre, which many see as the holiest of Christian shrines.

This huge limestone church was built on land given by Sultan Abdulaziz of the Ottoman Empire (which at that time was in control of these areas) to the German Kaiser, Wilhelm I. This seems to be another case of it's not <u>what</u> you know but <u>who</u> you know. The present church has German origins, hence being called *die Erlöserkirche*. The church was built over the site of the twelfth century Crusader Church of St Maria Latina. This isn't surprising for most buildings in the Holy Land are built on the site or over the remains of an earlier construction. It was dedicated on Reformation Day in 1898 and today is the home to a multi-lingual group of Protestant Christians. Services are conducted in Arabic, Danish, English and German.

But enough history. The tour group has come here to worship and not to be given a history lesson. Masoud with his impeccable driving skills got them to the church on time and they filed in full of expectation. Some were a little disappointed that the service was held in a smaller side chapel rather than the main church. No matter. It's the Word not the where, and the side chapel was lovely.

Colin had taken a seat in the second back row of pews for he wanted to get a few photographs. Then Judy Waller, who had taken the back pew with her husband, tapped him on the shoulder and asked, 'Is this really a Lutheran church?'

'Yes,' he assured her. 'Why do you ask?'

'Well,' she explained, 'the front pews were filled first and there is an ordained female Pastor, a woman Pastor.'

'No not the typical Lutheran church we are used to, but this is Jerusalem, Judy,' Colin answered with a smile, 'not Australia!'

Then the service progressed following a liturgical format with which they were quite familiar — except for the occasional foreign insertion such as *Yarabba ssalami amter alayna ssalam*. But it was great for everyone to be worshipping with folk from around the world, communing with them, united in a similar Christian faith. And what made it all the more poignant was that they were gathered here in the land where Jesus also worshipped and where today they were surrounded by people of the Moslem and Jewish faiths. Here the unity of humankind should be felt.

And had Jesus been there in person, surely he would have given his nod of approval to what he was hearing. Listening to Pastor Carrie's address he would have been shaking his head in disbelief in what he was hearing from the pulpit. Not that he would disagree with anything she said but that she needed to repeat the same message which he was giving two thousand years ago.

'Oh, you thick-headed people! Didn't you get the message I was trying to give you those many years ago? I came trying to break down barriers — well, social ones mainly — and here you are erecting high walls, walls to exclude and not to include. My message of love did not exclude people but embraced them.' Tears would run down his face as his head sadly moved.

What is it with powerful people and walls? Take the example involving the U.S.

President Donald Trump which the media enjoyed bringing to the attention of the world. Mr Trump stated during his candidacy announcement speech in 2015: "I will build a great wall — and nobody builds walls better than me, believe me — and I'll build them very inexpensively. I will build a great wall on the southern border, and I will make Mexico pay for that wall. Mark my words." Is he, and other wall builders, so blinkered by megalomania that they have not been able to see the lessons which history has to offer on walls?

Mr Trump wants to keep people **out** of his country. History well remembers Berlin in the 1960s, a few years after the Berlin wall had been built. The East German leader, Walter Ulbricht, in collaboration with the Soviet President, Nikita Khrushchev, wanted to wall the people **in**. They wanted to stop the people leaving their homeland. They billed it as an Anti-Fascist Protection Wall to keep western influences out of communist East Germany. Few would disagree however that this Wall of Shame, as West Berlin's Mayor, Willy Brandt, called it, was purely to imprison the East Berliners. A name cannot hide an intent.

That wall lasted fewer than thirty years. The few bits and pieces that remain today attract some curious, history-orientated tourists, and serve as a reminder to the stupidity of attempting to imprison populations.

It could also be argued that the Great Wall of China is experiencing, only in recent decades, its main effect on China, many hundreds of years after its construction. And it is drawing people to the country as tourists rather than trying to deny them entry as was its original purpose.

Walls seem to be built strongly into the psyche and written emphatically into the history of the people of Israel. It appears ever since the Israelites set foot into this area they have had a thing with walls. Around 1200 BCE after crossing the Jordan River from Moab at the end of their desert wanderings they were confronted by the city of Jericho, the gateway to Canaan. And the city was surrounded by a wall.

To push on into Canaan, to their planned destination, they would have to move through Jericho territory. Jericho would have to be defeated to have this access. But it was heavily defended. Joshua, the Leader of the Israelites, lay siege to the city, as the writer of the Book of Joshua wrote (Joshua 6:1): *Now Jericho was tightly shut up because of the Israelites. No one went out and no one came in.* We are not told how long the siege lasted because immediately following is the remarkable story of the walls of Jericho collapsing in the face of the Israelite processions. This surely should have been an indication to the Israelites that walls do not achieve their stated purpose. They represent merely an annoying impediment in the onward march of history.

Jerusalem also has often been defined by walls. It is interesting how today archaeologists are endeavouring to determine the exact location of the various walls in Jerusalem's history — the first wall, the second wall, the Turkish wall, the third wall. None of these, history enlightens, was able to achieve its primary purpose. Yes, they all came tumbling down.

Now on their travels through these ancient biblical lands the tourist again can see walls being erected. What an unsightly structure was seen when passing from the Palestinian lands around Bethlehem to Jewish Israel. How can this six-metre-high blight on the landscape be justified? This was the Israeli West Bank Separation Barrier. It was being built, as those in power claim, to protect Israeli citizens from attacks by Palestinian extremists. Others have called it an Apartheid Wall, a segregation wall. Is Israel creating a ghetto for itself? Not only will it be a 700-kilometre monstrosity running through the countryside, many in the world see it as a blight also on the integrity of the Israeli nation.

History tells us that it also will not fulfil its purpose.

Mr Netanyahu, tear down those walls! Make friends and not enemies.

The congregation seated in the Church of the Redeemer was hearing how the Word of God cannot be chained, cannot be walled in. In spite of political and anti-Christian powers in the world attempting to build walls of fear around the Gospel's principles of love, peace, justice and regard for creation, they will not succeed. They were reminded how workers for the Gospel were often being mocked and persecuted while the voices of division and racism seemed to be tolerated and accepted. Here in the Middle East, in the middle of political unrest, the peaceful atmosphere, and the message of peace and tolerance found within the limestone walls of this nineteenth century church spelt out an alternative direction for the world.

They came out of the church to the cup of tea table reassured once again that the Word of God is not chained. Walls may be built around people as well as around God's message, but they will suffer the same fate as those walls at Jericho and at Berlin, as those in China and in the United States.

*Don't fence me in!*

## Chapter 14

# Jericho

It seemed different. The mood of each and everyone appeared to be lifted. It was noticeable, and Sarah turned to Gordon and commented on what she noticed. 'There seems to be an air of expectation on the bus.'

They had just boarded the bus after attending the Sunday church service and today's journey would see them making their way through Jericho, north along the Jordan Valley to Galilee where they would stay in a lakeside hotel in Tiberius.

'Yes, I agree,' replied Gordon. 'Everyone seems a little more excited than usual.'

'What on earth did the pastor talk about in church to get everyone in this frame of mind?' Sarah, as an Israeli citizen, followed the Jewish faith and had not attended the Christian church with the members of the travelling group.

'I can't see how her message would have caused this reaction. On the contrary, her address gave us all something to think about. She talked about all the walls which are being built throughout the country. But despite that everyone does seem to be lifted. And it's not just a few.'

"Walls?' asked Sarah. 'What about the walls?'

'Well,' began Gordon, who realised he might be on shaky ground, 'it wasn't specifically about walls but rather how God's Word cannot be held in by walls. I do think however that...'

At this point Pastor Paul's clear, loud voice sounded throughout the bus. *'Joshua fit the battle of Jericho, Jericho, Jericho.'* Then he was joined by a few of the others. *'Joshua fit the battle of Jericho, and the walls came tumbling down.'*

A repetition of this verse had the majority of the passengers singing, louder and louder. Then the pastor continued in solo, *'You may talk about the men of Gideon, Yeah! You may talk about the men of Saul,'* Here everyone emphasised the "Yeah!" Pastor Paul continued, *'But there's none like good old Joshua, at the battle of Jericho.'* His invitation to join in followed and the well-known spiritual song rocked the bus as it made its way down to Jericho.

Singing finished, Pastor Paul returned to his seat. Sarah leaned across and asked him, 'Why the high spirits this morning?'

'I think the people see the tour as moving on now. No, not that they have not been enjoying it so far. Far from it. I've heard no bad reports, but a number have said to me how they are looking forward to seeing the Sea of Galilee.'

Now like the traveller in Jesus' parable of the Good Samaritan they were journeying down from Jerusalem to Jericho. And with Jerusalem located at around 750 metres above sea level and Jericho in the Jordan Valley lying 260 metres below sea level they were indeed journeying down.

Jericho lies in a particularly interesting landform — a rift valley known as the Jordan Rift Valley. Features such as this are located in very unstable regions of the world where gigantic tectonic plates are either rubbing together or pulling apart. As a result, these are areas where earthquakes and volcanic activity are regular occurrences. It's hard to realise that this countryside which appears so stable and solid, has experienced many devastating earthquakes throughout recorded history. These have been natural phenomena which have completely reduced towns and cities to heaps of rubble.

Archaeologists have claimed that Jericho appears to have been reconstructed at least twenty times in its long history because of what regularly happens. In spite of this ever-present danger, citizens have continued to resettle here, for springs of water emerging from the bordering hills have created an oasis in the dry surroundings. It is not surprising that Jericho had often been referred to as the city of palms.

As the bus drove into this scattered Palestinian settlement the palm trees were there to wave welcome. But the town was not the town through which Jesus passed. It was not the green oasis at which the pleading blind man could marvel after being touched by Jesus' healing hand. Nor was it the town from which the wealthy tax collector extorted his ill-gotten gains. Masoud, the driver, drove slowly past a sycamore tree but few were convinced it was the one climbed by Zacchaeus. Its name remained the same but here was a town struggling into the twenty-first century.

Somewhat like Jesus' visit many years ago, the group came and passed through Jericho on its way to somewhere else. They came here for it was the bottom end-station of the cable car which ran up to the Greek Orthodox Monastery situated half way up the side of the Mount of Temptation. This was the magnet which drew visitors to Jericho.

The bus had stopped and the passengers were milling around before heading to the transport which would swing them up to the traditional site of Jesus' temptation. Sarah joined Andrew who was sitting on one of the limestone seats beside a bubbling fountain, the Elisha Spring Fountain. For him this was a haven of peace, sitting in the cool shade of the date palms listening to the trickling water.

'You seem far away,' she began. 'A penny for your thoughts. Do you in Australia still say that even though you have dollars and cents?'

Andrew looked up and smiled. 'Well I do, anyway. A cent for your thoughts doesn't have the same pleasant rhythm as a penny.

It's lovely and peaceful here. I was thinking how much I've been enjoying this trip.'

'Oh, I had the impression that you were disappointed with some of the places we have been to so far. And let's face it, you have seemed so withdrawn and grumpy at times.'

'That's true. I was probably just a little bit tired; but other aspects are compensating for that.'

'Really? And could I ask what some of these other aspects might be?' asked Sarah.

'Well,' began Andrew, 'there's the encouragement everyone is showing me when they realise I have some health problems. It's as though they want to make this a very happy last innings for me.'

'Last innings. Don't be silly.'

'And with you especially... How shall I put it and not embarrass myself too much? I feel that...'

At that point when Andrew hesitated, Sarah reached out and placed her hand over his. He still didn't know what to say, so he said nothing. He looked away. Where? He looked up through the palm branches to the blue sky. He saw the doctor in his pale blue shirt with the yellow tie. It was he who delivered the bad news at that time. He didn't know what to say then either. There on the chair in the hospital he also had sat and looked blankly.

Now, as then, he was trying to clarify the emotion he was experiencing. Then it was shock and sadness. Was it now sexual? Heaven forbid! On a pilgrimage to the Holy Land where all the talk had been about Jesus and his love for us? What was the word? Agape. Yes, that's it. Agape. So far from the behaviour condemned in the sixth commandment. Can his reactions be only sexual?

He faltered. No, his were not unchaste feelings. Don't stop and analyse the pros and cons of reacting this way or that. Speak from your heart. Tell her that you are feeling deep affection for her. Tell her how you feel when she is addressing the group or when you watch her walking along. Tell her how her hair shines in the sun, how her eyes sparkle when she laughs. Tell her how you are always thinking about her. Tell her that you are falling in love with her.

No, she will not laugh at you. She will not ridicule your feelings. Whatever you might say, however you might sound when saying it, you cannot remain silent. You must tell Sarah how you feel.

Andrew raised his downcast eyes, preparing to express his feelings. 'Sarah,' he began, 'there is something that I really must...'

'Hello, you two,' interrupted Tony. 'Sarah, you're just the person I've been looking for. I've asked Gordon, but he suggested I come to you.'

Sarah jerked around at the sound of Tony's voice. 'Oh, it's you Tony. What did you say?'

'I said Gordon suggested I come and ask you.'

'Well, I'm all ears, Tony. How can I help you?'

'It's about Jericho,' began Tony.

'Yes? We are in the right place here to talk about Jericho,' said Sarah with a smile. 'What is it about Jericho you are so anxious to know?'

'A few months ago, a mate and I attended a fund-raising trivia night. One question — which is the oldest city in the world? — I thought I had nailed. Jericho. Wrong. The quizmaster gave the answer as Damascus. Naturally I appealed and put up a bit of a stink but to no avail. He maintained that his Googling had come up with Damascus. Now look at that.' And Tony pointed to the nearby fountain on which was written; **Jericho. The oldest city of the World.**

'Heavens, I'm no expert,' replied Sarah, 'but to save argument, and because we are actually here, let's go with Jericho being the oldest. I'll leave it to the historians and archaeologists for further investigation. Right now, I suppose it's about time we move to the cable-car terminus.'

'Lead on, my Guide. Lead me to temptation,' joked Tony with a bow and a wave of his arm.

## Chapter 15

# Temptation

In a couple brief sentences the Gospel of Mark (1:12-13) makes reference to Jesus being tempted by the Devil in the desert: *At once the Spirit sent him out into the desert, and he was in the desert forty days, being tempted by Satan. He was with the wild animals and angels attended him.*

Not only Mark, but also Matthew and Luke have recorded that after Jesus was baptised he spend time alone in the desert preparing for his ministry. This follows a pattern in Scriptures, readily recognised, where people spend time in the desert being strengthened and tested for what lies ahead.

Moses spent the second forty years of his life shepherding his father-in-law's sheep in the desert around Horeb, the Mountain of the Lord. This prepared him for the next, and his last, forty years when he guided the Israelites in their wanderings, again in the desert, to reach the promised land of Israel. The Apostle Paul also spent a number of years in the desert of Arabia after his conversion and before he started on his missionary journeys. Elijah, too, searched for God in the solitude of the deserts. Now, before beginning his life's mission, the gospel writers have Jesus preparing himself mentally for what was to follow.

Few would dispute the consensus that we do not really know to where he was led (Matthew & Luke) or sent (Mark). Tradition has it that he spent this time in a cave half way up a mountain which overlooks the town of Jericho. This general location seems logical enough, for the baptism apparently took place close by, in the Jordan River basically east of Jericho. Assuming he wanted to stay within the borders of his homeland, west of Jericho would fill the bill.

After taking the sky road up to the Greek Orthodox Monastery which is built around that Jesus cave there was a general reaction: This isn't really a desert location where one is away from it all. What a great view. It goes right across the Jordan valley and down to the Dead Sea. Surely this would have been a distraction for Jesus in his meditations. Sitting alone, hunger pains biting, the green, inviting oasis of Jericho would not have helped in the effort of working out God's ultimate plan for him. One could imagine him thinking: Where did that caravan come from? What are those priests doing? Whose donkey is that? Those people are working on the Sabbath. Look at all the date palms.

But it is usually accepted that one must be advised by tradition. For centuries this mount has been known as Mt Quadrantania (Latin for forty). Locating Jesus' desert experience here goes back to Byzantine times.

'What a great view. Great photos waiting for me here,' enthused Colin running around taking a few shots every time he stopped. 'But I'll tell you something. I'm pleased I didn't have to walk up here.'

'I agree, Colin,' said Pastor Paul. 'It was bad enough zigzagging up those steps on the cliff face to get here from where the lift finished, let alone having to walk the whole way.'

'I found it scary just looking over the side of the steps,' Pastor Paul's wife, Julie, added. 'You wouldn't want to be scared of heights if you had to live up here.'

'Yes, and remember what Phillip told us about all the earthquakes that occur in this area.' Tony had joined the discussion and wanted to add a little drama. 'Suppose one hit now while we are all up here. Rumble, rumble. Shake, shake. Scream, scream, and we'd be back down in Jericho in no time flat.'

'Nice one, Tony; but let's assume that won't happen and we can go on and enjoy these interesting, old painted walls.' And he was off with his Canon EOS something-or-other, making sure no painting escaped his lens.

Tony then turned to Pastor Paul, ' Well, here we are halfway up to temptation. What do you think, Pastor Paul? Do you really think that Jesus spent forty days and forty nights up here in this cave wrestling with the Devil?'

'That's a good question, Tony,' Paul replied, and then hesitated.

'Well?'

'In this particular cave, one can't be sure. We are relying on tradition and this could be based on incorrect information. I do believe that Jesus would have spent long hours agonising over his calling in life. And it makes sense that he would go into the solitude of a desert to do this. For forty days? Probably just a general term meaning quite a long time. And the wrestling? I believe that was in his mind and was not a physical encounter.'

Tony could see that Avril and Margaret were standing to the side but listening intently to what was being said. At one stage, seeing the surprised and questioning look on Avril's face, he sensed that they were about to interrupt; but they held back. He then put his next question. 'OK, assuming it may not have been this cave, what are we doing here then?'

'Well, it could act as an incentive for you to go back and look up the biblical record of this event in Jesus' life.'

'Fair enough, I might just do that,' agreed Tony. 'But did I need to come all this way to get that prod?'

'Perhaps not, but being in the geographic location adds another dimension to our study of the Word.'

'Assuming that this was the location,' commented Tony a little sarcastically. 'I think we are going around in circles. I might catch up with Margaret and Avril and give them some guidance.'

That night after dinner, Andrew had gone straight back to his room to catch up on his diary writing. Tony said he would go into the saloon and find someone to join him in having a few beers. Andrew had hardly begun writing when Tony turned up back in their room.

'What, no luck?' asked Andrew looking up from his diary.

'I don't know. What's wrong with everyone?'

'No one there?'

'No, only a few from our group. I thought for sure Colin and probably Phillip and Kaye would be there; but they weren't,' said a disappointed Tony.

'What about that couple and their daughter?'

'No such luck. They seem to keep to themselves most of the time.'

'Who was there then?'

'Well, there were those two couples who were arguing down at the Dead Sea. They must have solved their problems for they certainly were not arguing in there. Two of them were at one table with their heads in a Bible discussing something. The short fellow and the other chap's wife.'

'And the other two?'

'They were sitting in the lounge area with their drinks, laughing and having a great time. It would have been rude for me to interrupt them. So here I am.'

He sat down and turned on the TV. He began flicking around the channels looking for one that spoke English. Not finding anything to his liking he surprised Andrew with a suggestion, 'Why don't we look up those temptation of Jesus stories in the Bible and see what they really have to say about Mt Temptation?'

## Chapter 15  Temptation

'Are you serious?' Andrew hardly believed that this suggestion would come from Tony.

'Sure. Nothing on TV. Time for some good old-fashioned Bible study. But we will have to use your Bible. I didn't bring one.'

'That's OK. We should be able to manage that. I've just begun writing up my diary for the day, but that can wait.'

They were soon considering what Matthew, Mark and Luke had to say about the temptation.

'This takes me back a few years,' remarked Andrew. 'Just like those Bible study sessions we used to go to when we were in the youth group at church.'

'Don't remind me of those,' Tony was quick to reply. 'Do you remember Adam? He was a real pain in the arse.'

'Yes, I remember him, but why do you say that?'

'Well,' answered Tony, 'whenever I wanted to throw in a few logical, theological ideas which he didn't agree with he would point to his Bible and say: "But in my Bible it says that..." He would not listen to my logic.'

'Don't be too hard on him. He had his ideas and was a sincere sort of a fellow. I wonder what he's up to now?'

'No idea. I bet he, Avril and Margaret would get along well together.'

'Tony, don't be getting at those two so often. Don't spoil this trip for them.'

'Get away with you. They enjoy it. They like a bit of arguing.'

'Anyway,' said Andrew as he pointed to his Bible on the table in front of them, 'let's leave Adam and our two travelling companions and see what my Bible has to say about the temptation.'

'Funny!'

'We shall now determine if it says the same to me as it says to you.'

For the next hour the two friends delved into the secrets of the Bible — comparing and contrasting the three accounts of Jesus' temptation.

Then Andrew conceded, 'You know, we could go on and on. But we probably are just nitpicking and missing the main point of the story.'

Tony replied, 'No argument from me there. And I agree; the forty, the three and being in the desert, these are themes which come up again and again in the Bible. I think it's a sure sign that we are not to take those stories literally. Instead we should focus on the real meaning of the story.'

'So, what is the main point of this story?' Andrew wanted to know.

'I'll leave that to Pastor Paul. But I wonder. Did climbing, oops, I mean taking the chair lift to Mt Quadrantania, get me any closer to the main point?'

'Oh, go to bed! And it wasn't a chair lift. It was a cable car.'

\* \* \*

## Extract from Andrew's travel diary:

I have been sitting here on the balcony of our room rethinking what I might have said to Sarah today instead of being dumb. (What? Tony is back already.)

At work and then in the seminar room at the Theological Academy I was never stuck for something to say. No matter how worked up I might have been I would never let my emotions get the better of me. But today, when Sarah put her hand over mine something spread through me. I became mentally paralysed.

I felt myself blushing and I could see that she also had a moment of embarrassment. What would have happened if Tony

## Chapter 15  Temptation

had not come on the scene at that moment? No, not what would have happened, but what might we have said?

I could sit here and sketch out a composition. With time to think, I could write down what I would like to say in a situation like the one I was experiencing today. And I would have Sarah say the things which I would like to hear from her.

Probably I should be more like Tony and speak what I feel without worrying about where it might lead or the reaction it might provoke.

Tony spoilt what could have been the right moment today. When will the next moment come along? Who knows.

Maybe I should create the moment; but would that be the right thing to do on a tour such as this? Is a pilgrimage the right place for a holiday romance? Well a half-holiday romance now that it is half over. There is only a week to go and I don't want to have my time here spoilt by having my pent-up emotions crying out for release.

We visited Mt Temptation today, the traditional site where Jesus wrestled with his emotions, deciding which path to follow. Yes, we all must make decisions.

*Looking down on the Palestinian town of Jericho from Mt Temptation.*

## Chapter 16

# On the Sea of Galilee

The blue, morning waters of the Sea of Galilee offered an open invitation to all: Come and share your day with me.

Gordon's Aussie party of pilgrims had eagerly looked forward to being in Jesus' home district and especially to their trip on the Sea, many feeling that it would be the highlight of their journey to the Holy Land. The time had finally arrived. There was a spring in their steps and smiles on their faces as they were welcomed on board their boat by Captain Daniel. The excitement mounted.

Soon the *Faith Boat 71526* was effortlessly ferrying its passengers to their designated destination. In doing this it was enacting what had been happening on this body of water for millennia; boats moving people from place to place. It is even mentioned in the Bible that Jesus would hop into a boat to get to the other side of the lake. In this instance, however, the actual fact of being on the water was the prime purpose of this trip for the passengers, rather than arriving at some jetty in the distance. Even though this was the case, the tour organisers had decided that in the interest of efficiency, the smooth running of a tour itinerary and seeing an interesting object related to these waters, the end station was also relevant. There would be something very interesting to be seen there. But first the sea journey was beginning.

No unexpected storm had appeared over the horizon to upset the waters. They remained untroubled and friendly. The sky was cloudless, painted in a pale, relaxing shade of blue. The mid-morning sun played on the rippled surface creating endless rows of sparkles. Here was peace. Here was joy.

The hotel buildings had already disappeared, swallowed up by the dun-coloured hillsides. The hazy, grey bulk of the Golan Heights loomed away to the east. Seen from the water solely as a landform and not an area of troubled, political wrangling, it provided a neutral backdrop to the peacefulness of the lake. The *Faith Boat 71526* was by itself but not alone. Other craft loaded with other pilgrim groups also experiencing this calmness of the Sea of Galilee silently slipped past following their own particular course. Here was contentment. Here was happiness.

They were well out onto the lake when guide Sarah called for the attention of all members of the group and addressed them. 'Isn't this beautiful? Let's say ten more minutes for you to finish your chatting or your quiet enjoyment of the sea and then your Captain and I have something special planned for you.'

'Is it what I think it is?' asked Colin with a smile on his face and a twinkle in his eye.

'Well, I can't really answer that, Colin. I have no idea what you are thinking,' replied Sarah. 'I suppose you will just have to wait and be surprised. Oh, and when I say I have something planned for you, I mean ALL of you, even you up there, pretending that you are not listening to me!'

Andrew was sitting in the bow of the boat looking out over the quiet rippling of the water; pensive, his thoughts idly drifting. The sound of a small group quietly singing, guided by Simon's ukulele, and others in discussion, were gently breaking the quiet of the still waters, but not disturbing his meditation. Clearly everyone was enjoying the experience of being on these waters. But he sat alone, contemplating the sea's existence and what it evoked. His mind was alive.

He thinks: Jesus sailed on these waters.

But then: These waters? These actual waters?

He smiles and has to agree with himself that they were not really these waters. The waters of Jesus' time have long since disappeared, drawn up by the thirsty summer sun, harvested to irrigate sagging crops or seduced down to a salty grave in the Dead Sea. I'm sure Phillip would agree with me on that. Maybe he should have given us a lesson on the Sea of Galilee too.

And then he wonders: Does my lay-man's understanding of the natural water cycle lessen my appreciation of what I see before me? For many this is but a lake, a basin of fresh, clear water. It supports life in and around it. It is undeniably a great blessing to the region. The fishermen depend on it to provide their catch. The crops of the farmers would die without it. The tourist hotels would serve no purpose standing alone without the lake. All of this would justify its existence. But for many others this is much more than a fresh-water lake.

Resting here on a boat in the fresh, cool of the morning it is easy to see the physical appeal of the place. But I can feel more. For a Christian it is impossible not to feel some emotional appeal which pervades the lake. I'm sure not only I, but all members of the group will remember these moments alone with one's own thoughts and the perceived presence of the Lord.

Yes, one has to include the Lord. For the Christian, the presence of the Lord is indeed still here. Sure, I remember at the Academy, Doctor, whichever one it was, saying how the Lord is present wherever one may be. And then he added, probably for my benefit: "Yes, even in Queensland." And I cheekily replied, "You mean **especially** in Queensland, don't you Doctor?" The lake here in Jesus' homeland heightens our perception of his continuing presence. Sitting here, quietly, I feel that his presence penetrates my soul. He becomes part of me.

I ask myself whether I am drawn closer to the Lord by this

experience. I am thinking but am finding this a difficult question to answer. For me, it's hard to say. Is it because of my illness and the distraction this always causes whatever the situation? It makes me more aware of my mortality. I feel that I will not have the opportunity to communicate to others any deep perception of feeling close to God. To me this would be an empty, inappropriate emotion in the presence of others who are showing happiness and contentment.

What about from the other point of view. Has the Lord drawn closer to me in this place in my need? I certainly hope so.

Thinking about Jesus, it's easy to see why he left his hometown of Nazareth and came down here — to Capernaum — to live. I remember being up there a few days ago; hot, barren, hilly. Not the best place in the world to live. Then he came down here; cool, fertile, enjoyable. A place which enhances life. Reminds me of the people in Queensland who move to the Gold Coast or Sunshine Coast to live. But there is a difference, I suppose. Most move to the coast in Queensland to retire, their life's work basically behind them. Jesus came here to get on with his calling. He came here to recharge his batteries, to be with his fishing friends, giving them guidance and purpose for their lives, to help them in their struggles.

What about my newly-acquired friends in the boat here with me? They, and I, will move on when this boat reaches its destination and when our plane finally takes us back home. Some will have to go back to their jobs. Others will continue their retirement, no doubt enriched by their experiences here. For each of us will have discovered in our own unique way, that Jesus' presence has remained here. His foot-prints are still on the water.

'Hello. Can I interrupt?' Sarah had been watching Andrew for some time and now approached him. 'You seemed so far away. Were you back in Australia?'

## Chapter 16  On the Sea of Galilee

Andrew looked up awakened from his daydreaming, saw Sarah and smiled.

'Anything but,' he replied. 'I was seduced by this place and my thoughts were out there on the water, bouncing around from one ripple to another, as it were.'

'It appeared that this saddened you rather than lifted your spirits.'

Andrew looked into Sarah's sincere, sympathetic eyes, opened his mouth to speak, but no words emerged. He clasped his hands to help gain control of his emotions. Sarah leaned across and enclosed his hands in hers.

'Oh, Andrew,' she began. 'I... I...' but was unable to continue, realising that she was going down a pathway which could prove to be very difficult for both Andrew and herself. Then, releasing his hands and looking away, she blurted out, 'Do you go fishing back home?'

'Fishing? Do I go fishing?' Andrew was stunned back to reality. 'What on earth prompted that question?'

'I'm sorry,' stammered Sarah. 'I don't know. It's probably because I saw that fishing boat over there and that's what came out.'

'No. I haven't been fishing for years. My dad used to take me down to the local creek when I was a kid and we would catch eels and Jew fish, and...'

'Jew fish?' interrupted Sarah, proud of her Israeli heritage.

'Yes, Jew fish. That's what everyone called them,' answered Andrew.

'Why on earth is a fish called a Jew fish?' Sarah wanted to know.

'No idea. It has never crossed my mind that the name has anything to do with the Jewish people,' Andrew said. 'Never really thought about. Everyone called them Jew fish and that's all there was to it. Maybe you should google it.'

'So, you have never been a fisherman and now you are studying to become a fisher of men? Isn't that what Jesus called some of his fishermen friends here around the lake?'

'Yes, that's what it says in the Gospels. But with my illness that will probably never happen. But let's not go there Sarah, or I'll become very morbid again. This is too lovely a day and too beautiful a place for me to spoil it for myself.' Andrew was already finding the words starting to stick in his throat.

'I'm sorry.' Sarah realised she should not have said something which might cause Andrew to think about his illness. 'But come with me,' she brightened, taking his hand in a cheerful, comradely manner. 'We are all about to learn some lively Israeli dances and you, my friend, are not getting out of it!'

## Chapter 17

# Ancient Galilee Boat

ON THE SHORE OF LAKE TIBERIUS, CIRCA 30 CE:

The sky above the mountain block to the east was signalling the beginning of a new day but the turbulent waters of the lake were still black and foreboding. The restlessness of the dark waters remained unabated, still troubled by the whistling wind. Cold, wet and tired, the members of the crew of the fishing boat were dragging their heavy vessel across the pebbly sand beyond the reach of the waves.

No one spoke. The dull moan of the wind and the irregular splash of the waves on the shore were interrupted from time to time by the grunting of heaving men and the occasional expletive as one lost his footing and fell to his knees to be washed by the relentless waves. The men were strong, but the load was heavy.

These hardened fishermen had spent their lives learning the ways of the water. Many claimed to be able to smell the location of a shoal of profitable fish, but they also acknowledged the forces of nature which were unleashed when the lake was angry. During this past night it had become angry. At these times fighting was pointless, indeed impossible. Best then to rescue the nets, make for the shore, touch solid land and escape the clutches of a watery death.

The task on this dreary pre-dawn was daunting but the men persevered. They pulled. They struggled. They would not tolerate defeat. Finally, with the boat secure, the weary fishermen were seated around a stuttering fire. It was having difficulty driving the wet and cold from the tired bodies. The conversation was about their night's activities.

'Could have bloody-well drowned out there last night,' was Yakov's candid assessment of the night's fishing. 'And where on earth did that storm come from?'

'Who knows,' replied Aaron, who was the owner of the boat. 'There was no indication when we set out. And it came down from the hills so quickly. It was on us before I knew what was happening.'

'I'll tell you something,' came in Ben. 'The fish must have known it was coming. They certainly went off into hiding. We should have dropped to it when our nets were continually coming up empty. Should have headed back home then.'

'You're right,' agreed Yakov. 'Nearly losing our lives for what? Two lousy, bloody fish. That's not going to pay the taxes for the boss let alone put food into our stomachs.'

'No one would disagree with you there, Yakov. It's getting harder and harder. You know as well as I that last night with the storm wasn't the only time we've caught basically nothing. It's happening more and more often,' the owner and captain said with a shake of his head. 'I don't know how we will keep going.'

'How **we** will keep going,' Yakov came back. 'I think the big problem is whether the old boat will keep going. Nearly busted my gut pulling the old bugger out of the water this morning. She was almost half full of water. Another plank must have come loose or simply dropped off. If it was up to me I would have left the damned thing out there to sink.'

'Great. But what about us? Go down with it? And yes, I agree with you. We will have to look at the damage later,' agreed Aaron.

'And we had better have a good look at the mast,' said Ben. 'There was a lot of bending and cracking in it last night. How's that grog holding out? I can't for the life of me warm up.'

## Chapter 17  Ancient Galilee Boat

Life for the fishermen on the Sea of Galilee (Lake Tiberius) had never been easy; battling nature's elements, outwitting the elusive shoals, catching enough to feed family and a hungry tax system. In the last years it had become even more difficult. When asked why, all would point to the local ruler, their Tetrarch Herod Antipas, and his ambitions.

When his father, King Herod the Great died in 4 BCE, Antipas hoped to follow in his father's footsteps. This did not happen. Herod's large kingdom was divided between his three sons. Antipas was not even granted rulership over the desired areas around Jerusalem which the Roman Emperor, Augustus, gave to Herod's son, Archelaus. Antipas was made tetrarch of the remote regions of Galilee and Perea.

Augustus died in 14 CE but Antipas' ambition to be the King of the Jews remained. He set about ingratiating himself with the new Roman Emperor, Tiberius. He remembered how his father had courted Augustus by building an imposing new capital city, Caesarea Maritima, on the Mediterranean coast. Antipas' capital was Sepphoris, a less than impressive city, located in the hill country of Galilee so he decided to build a more imposing capital to honour the current Emperor. This new city was to be built on the shores of the Sea of Galilee and so the newly-named Lake Tiberius was born and on its shores the city of Tiberius came into existence.

With the construction of this new expensive capital came pressure to squeeze more revenue out of the local industries, foremost being fishing. More fish had to be netted, longer hours had to be worked and fish stocks became depleted. The industry suffered. The fishermen suffered and became restless. All this so that Antipas could impress the emperor in Rome.

Many fishermen had to leave the only way of life they had ever known. What could they then do? Where could they go?

Aaron, his crew and their aging boat, remained and struggled to make a livelihood. Being caught in a storm did little to improve their situation. Later in the morning, Aaron and the others were assessing the damage sustained by the boat during the previous night. The light of mid-morning revealed the true physical damage.

'Good Lord,' said Yakov, 'we are damned lucky to be standing here alive. Look here will you. Where are the rudder mountings? The mast is cracked right through. And those bottom planks. What a bloody mess!'

'You're right,' Aaron had to admit. 'We have a real mess on our hands. But thank the Lord God for saving us. I remember what happed to that boat from Magdala which was caught in a similar storm last year. The poor beggars didn't stand a chance.'

'So, what now?' young Joseph wanted to know. 'We can't go out on a boat in this condition, and it will be out of action for Goodness knows how long. What are we going to do?'

'What can we do?' a worried Ben wanted to know. 'Join the crowds standing around the village well waiting for some day work? All they do is grumble. It's easy to see why. Not many end up getting a day's work.'

'Tell you what I'm going to do,' said Yakov. 'I've been hearing a lot about a preacher man going around who seems to be on our side. At least a lot of out-of-work fishermen have been following him around. They say he's planning some sort of peaceful revolution.'

'A peaceful revolution?' asked Aaron. 'What that? Revolutions can't be peaceful. The only thing the old schemer knows is force. He is not going to lower our taxes simply by being nice to him. That's not how our rulers work.'

'It won't hurt to tag along for a while and see what he has to offer,' said Yakov. 'I believe he comes from around Capernaum, so he shouldn't be too hard to track down.'

'I'm sure the old fox, Antipas, would be able to track him

down as well if he's talking about revolution, peaceful or not. So, I'd be careful if I were you. With all this unrest around, put a foot wrong and you will be in trouble,' Aaron remarked. 'In the meantime, I'll see what I can have done with my boat. She's had plenty of repairs before, so a few more would probably be possible. I will take it to the yard and let them have a look at the damage. But if it's not worth while… I'll wait and see.'

---

And so, with the passengers singing, dancing or just sitting and thinking, the *Faith Boat* arrived at its destination. It slowly bumped into position alongside the short wooden pier which served the needs of the Kibbutz Ginosar. Crowding noisily on the pier watching the arrival was a colourful band of pilgrims waiting their turn to travel on Galilee's enticing waters.

'Hey! Where are you people from?'

'Australia,' was shouted back from a variety of friendly voices still on board.

'Australia. Aussie, hey? Aussie Aussie Aussie. Oi Oi Oi!'

Clearly this group had come across compatriots from the land down under. Good manners and curiosity dictated that a similar question should be asked of this elated group. The answer was loud and clear.

'Ghana! Yes, Ghana! Hallelujah!'

Tony turned to Andrew who was following him off the boat, 'Come now. A boisterous welcome of wide, white smiles like that must surely put you in a good mood.'

'Aren't they a happy crowd!' replied Andrew, risking a slight smile.

Dodging a 'Bless you, Brother' as he stepped onto the pier, Tony continued, 'You know, this reminds me of Neville Gordon back in Brisbane. You remember him?'

'Of course, from the footy club. He played with us a number of times but never did hold down a permanent spot in the firsts. Could never rely on him turning up for training. Why do you mention him?"

'Don't you remember his nick-name?'

'Sure, it was Gunna, but I don't see how Ghana... Oh, for heaven's sake Tony! I will never understand how your mind works. It looks like our group is headed for that tree over there.'

'Yes. You go on over and get a spot nice and close to Sarah. I'll be over in a little while. I'm Ghana take a few photos of those Hallelujahs and happy smiles.'

With a shake of his head, Andrew made his way over to the Australian flag fluttering under a pine tree.

'I see Gordon has described it as "The Jesus Boat" in the itinerary,' Sarah was speaking to the group, 'but that's probably just to get your attention. It's more accurately called The Ancient Galilee Boat. That name says it all without any emotion. You will be seeing the preserved remains of an actual old fishing boat which sailed here on the Sea of Galilee some 2000 years ago. And yes, you mathematicians are correct. That takes us back to the time when Jesus lived here. But that's all we can definitely say. I'll leave your imagination to fill in what might have happened during its working life. As I said, you will have time to see the remains in the museum here. Many, like myself, I must admit, don't get terribly excited about seeing these wooden remains. For me it's the journey which the boat had previously travelled, and which finally brought its remains here to Ginosar which excites me.'

'Do you have some secret knowledge, and really do know who originally owned the boat?' Kaye, the historian, wanted to know.

'No, Kaye, there is just no way of knowing. I suppose you could call it The Peter Boat, if you wanted to. He was one of

Jesus' followers, wasn't he? We must assume that he actually was a fisherman in those days.'

'What about The Philip Boat?' someone called from the back of the group.

'Perhaps the Zebedee Boat.'

'Who?'

'Zebedee. You know, the father of James and John. Doesn't it say somewhere that they were sitting in their father's boat mending the nets?'

Sarah tried to interrupt but was finding it difficult. For all that, she enjoyed sessions such as this, as it was very evident that the majority of the group had a very good knowledge of the Bible. She finally slipped in, 'Maybe it was The Mary Boat.' This called a halt to the other suggestions.

'Mary? But she was a woman.'

'Well spotted, Colin,' smiled Sarah in his direction. 'There is evidence that there were women in business back then. And it has been suggested that Mary from Magdala, just down the way a little from here, was involved in the fishing industry. I'm sure you will come up with some other ideas after you visit the museum. We will first be viewing the movie, and this will give you a good idea of the skill and care involved in bringing these wooden bones here. Take time to read the information in the display room for this will get your imagination working. You will then be able to ponder the mystery of the 2000-year old Galilee boat for yourselves.'

\* \* \*

The drought of 1985 in Israel had resulted in the volume of water in the Sea of Galilee decreasing markedly. Large areas near the shores which would normally be covered with relatively shallow water were exposed. A few kilometres north of Magdala, on the sea's north-west shore, the outline of a boat became visible in the mud. Luckily a couple of brothers from the Kibbutz Ginosar nearby, keen amateur archaeologists, recognised the outline for what it was. A very old boat. Here was a discovery that needed to be approached very professionally for it to be completely recovered without damage.

The necessary official archaeologists were notified and the site secured until experts could determine how best to rescue the boat from the muddy, watery grave. Not only recognised experts but also many of the residents became involved and the remains of the boat were soon exposed by this army of willing hands. The excitement among the experts grew for they saw something very old and very important emerging from the mud. It soon became clear that all care would need to be exercised so that no damage was done during the operation.

Once fully exposed the entire remains were enclosed in lightweight, solid materials which allowed them to be floated to an area on land for the preservation procedures to begin. It was taken to the museum site at Ginosar which had recently been built and here submerged in liquids which would help preserve it. After fourteen years soaking in a polyethylene glycol (PEG) the structure was stabilised and finally presented to the public.

Now groups or individuals were able to stand near the remains of this old boat and imagine its possible life when it was working on the water and not resting beneath the waves in its muddy grave.

So, can it reasonably be called The Jesus Boat? i.e. a fishing boat belonging to a friend of Jesus and on which he travelled. Was it the boat, or one of the many boats, by which Jesus moved around the region before and during his ministry? The Gospels give occasions when he would preach to the crowd from a boat because they were pushing to be near him (Luke 5:3). At other times he used a boat to move from one part of the area to another (Mark 6:53). Then there were times when he may have merely accompanied them on a fishing trip to get away from the crowds and have a little rest (Matthew 8:24).

The greater part of Jesus' ministry took place around the north-western segment of the sea. He had many friends who were associated with fishing and so it is *possible* that Jesus had sailed in this boat. But we will never know.

Another intriguing suggestion is that it was a fishing boat which was then used by the rebels in the Jewish uprising against the Romans in 66-72 CE. The local fishermen lived in a situation where they were severely oppressed by the ruling class, puppets of Rome, and many would have joined the rebel forces in a fight for freedom. Their boats would have been used to transport fighters and weapons around the area.

Did it see action in the battle of Migdal (Magdala) in 67 CE when the Roman legions led by future emperor, Vespasian, routed the local Jewish forces? There was a great loss of Jewish life, the countryside was laid waste and the Romans systematically destroyed the towns and villages. Severely damaged boats would have been used to repair the less-damaged. Once stripped these would have been left to sink near the shipyards. Was this one of these which saw action in this crippling war? If the boat was around at this time it would *most likely* have been involved in the uprising.

Various dating techniques — radiocarbon dating, matching pottery pieces, analysing type of nails and the construction method — have placed the boat on the water between 80 BCE and 80 CE. The recovered remains of the boat contained at least ten different types of timber. This would seem to indicate a scarcity of materials or a struggling owner who could not afford the correct replacements. The boat itself had provision for four oars as well as a mast. All indicators seem to point to this being a fishing boat belonging to an individual who was struggling to make the business profitable. It seems *certain* then that this boat belonged to a fisherman who operated at or around the time of Jesus.

Now in its new life these 2000-year-old pieces of timber, previously assembled by someone showing remarkable craftsmanship, can transport its visitors back across the centuries to a time when Jesus may, or may not, have stepped or slept on them.

\* \* \*

Stephen and Frances Gersekowski did not immediately follow the others into the museum. Stephen had started to move off but Frances took his arm and held him back.

Stephen stopped and looked questioningly at her. 'What's the matter? What do you want?'

'You just can't help yourself, can you?' his wife said.

'Stephen frowned with a puzzled look on his face. 'What do you mean? What have I done now?'

'You know exactly what I am getting at. You and Judy Waller.'

'Me and Judy Waller? What are you talking about? You can't be serious. What exactly have I done this time to upset you like this?'

Frances was obviously becoming annoyed with her husband, who in her mind seemed to be playing dumb. 'I thought you would get the message after what happened down at the Dead Sea. But, no! Nothing seems to sink in with you.'

'Are you talking about on the boat? Just because I was doing some of those Israeli dances with her?' Stephen finally realised what his wife seemed to be upset about. 'Come on now. Everyone was just having a bit of fun.'

'It's how you and she were dancing. Much closer than others

seemed to be. But it's not only that. You still seem to be spending a lot of time together.'

'Well, what do you expect?' Stephen began in his defence. 'You and Gary always seem to have your heads together discussing some Bible text or other. And you know that I am not interested in those deep discussions. Judy isn't either. I should be complaining that you and he are spending too much time together.'

'Well, you know now how I feel,' said Frances ignoring what he had to say about her discussions with Gary Waller. 'We had better be going into the museum now to look at that boat. I see Gordon over there looking hard at us. If we are not careful, everyone will be talking about us.'

Stephen looked over and gave Gordon a wave. Then he took his wife's hand and they headed off together towards the present resting place of The Ancient Galilee Boat.

*No, not the Ancient Galilee Boat, but an abandoned craft in the boat harbour of Tiberius.*

Chapter 18

# Beatitudes

The morning had begun on a very high note. There was expectation and excitement in the air as the refreshed travellers climbed into the coach. Driver Masoud had to reply to as many "Good days" as on the first day. The reason was easy to understand. They were off to visit sites in and around Capernaum, Jesus' home town. This was the real Jesus country. It was here that those elusive footsteps of the Lord might be discerned and followed.

The coach might even be following some of the exact pathways once trodden by Jesus. The first of these probable pathways (now a roadway) was leading uphill from the sea shore at Tiberius.

The Gospel of Matthew 5:1-2 reads: *Now when he saw the crowds he went up on a mountainside and sat down. His disciples came to him and he began to teach them saying: Blessed are the poor in spirit...*

And so begins a well-known passage in the New Testament known as the Sermon on the Mount. This sermon begins with Jesus' eight pronouncements of blessedness, generally known as the beatitudes. Tradition has located the site of Jesus' sermon on a hill overlooking the Sea of Galilee. The coach was now winding its way up towards a chapel erected on this hill in commemoration of this episode, highlighting some basic principles of Jesus' teaching.

Did the passengers sitting in the air-conditioned comfort of the tour coach look out of the windows and picture Jesus and his disciples trudging slowly up the hill in the September heat? Some did, many didn't. Did they glance out and see the passing landscape scene? A few may have. One definitely did. Phillip, the geography teacher, looked nowhere else. He indeed, would be the first to admit that he was captivated by the landscape rather than by an image of Jesus and his followers making their way slowly along the dusty hillside.

Phillip looked and catalogued the countryside as it passed. He saw that they were now travelling through basalt country and that the limestone landscape around Jerusalem had been left far behind. The telltale piles of round, black boulders stood out in the pale, dry grass on the hillside. The road cuttings gave a clear view of the red-brown earth enfolding the decomposing basalt pieces. In the grass on the uncultivated steeper slopes individual black rocks scattered through the paddock seemed in Phillip's mind to be a flock of black sheep grazing the dry pasture.

The smooth curves of the hilltops were broken by the irregular outline of small bushy trees, their dark green rendered even darker, approaching black, against the light of the sky. The sky could have indeed been the doorway to heaven. It was without clouds, a vibrant blue of shining purity.

Looking downhill, the land changed. It became more human. The boulder-strewn grassland of the steeper slopes had become gently sloping cultivated fields. Blue-black stones no longer dotted the fields. They had been gathered in past generations and put to better use by being made into fences and buildings. The pale, red-brown soil lay silent awaiting the broadcaster with the seed. Other fields stood out in green. Here the date palms and olive trees grew in the fertile soil.

This could have been the setting which prompted Jesus to challenge his hearers with the parable of the Sower (Mark 4: 1-20). Here was the open pathway, the rocky, stony places, the growth of thorny shrubs and prickly thistles. Here also the fertile soil.

Whereas some of the pilgrims on the coach were driving

through the setting of an age-old parable, others were using the available WiFi facilities to read the latest news from home.

The coach had soon parked at the top of the hill and everyone had alighted and gathered under a shady tree to hear once again the eight beatitudes recorded in the Gospel of St Matthew. Pastor Paul had read the eight verses and then continued. 'You know, many colleagues of mine believe we should say that there are nine beatitudes, for the reading continues: *Blessed are you when people insult you, persecute you and falsely say all kinds of evil against you because of me.* Many would agree with them, but probably even more would disagree.'

'So why don't we say nine?' Avril wanted to know.

'When you look carefully at that ninth one, it seems unlikely that Jesus would have said anything like that during his ministry. He says how people were being persecuted because of him. But it was only after his execution and after the Jesus group, or let's say the Christian Church, had become established that his followers were severely persecuted.'

'What! Are you saying Jesus did not say that? It seems quite clear the way you read it that he did.' Avril seemed quite annoyed.

'Yes, it is possible that he did not,' replied the Pastor. 'Many Bible scholars today say that this extra beatitude was added by the writer of the Gospel to give some comfort to those who at that time were being persecuted. That was 40-50 years after Jesus had been killed.'

'Well I never,' replied Avril shaking her head. 'I never would have thought that I would hear something like that coming from a Pastor. It makes you think what other funny ideas some might have.'

At this stage of the discussion, Sarah, who had been standing to the side, came forward and defused what could have developed into an embarrassing situation.

'I'm sorry to butt in,' she started, 'but we really must keep moving. We shall meet in the chapel where I will give you a little information about the building. Then you will have time to stroll around the grounds and enjoy this lovely setting.'

With that she directed everyone into the Church of the Beatitudes and headed off in that direction herself.

Tony gave Andrew a nudge in the ribs. 'Come on,' he said, 'let's catch up to the peacemaker.'

They were soon walking beside Sarah who was reading through her notes. 'Peace,' said Tony raising his right hand with two fingers held high.

Sarah looked puzzled.

Andrew explained. 'Tony wants to thank you for keeping peace back there between Avril and Pastor Paul. Had you not...'

Tony butted in. 'Had you not moved us on we may have seen one of the highlights of the tour.'

'Tony, I don't for a moment believe you think like that. Anyway, wasn't one of those... what do you call them? Yes, that's right, beatitudes. Wasn't one, blessed are the peacemakers?'

'Oh, I'm sorry. My Mum has always said that I'm always causing trouble. Anyway, blessed be thou, O Sarah!'

Sarah blushed. 'How do you put up with him, Andrew? Doesn't he drive you crazy?'

'Yes, he embarrasses me quite often. That's a fact,' replied Andrew. 'But I've known him for a long time and I suppose I'm used to him by now. And underneath it all, he's not such a bad type really.'

'I suppose I'll have to take your word for that.' Sarah however, didn't seem convinced. 'But we must hurry. I have a church full of pilgrims waiting for me to tell them all about it. Now where are my notes?' She stopped and laughed. "You know, I sounded just like before when I interrupted Pastor Paul and Avril. Perhaps I'm trying to stop an argument here too.'

With that she left the two young men looking at one another.

She hurried on into the church. When they arrived a little later she already had the attention of the group.

Not only is the church located on a site which has an impressive vista across the Sea of Galilee to the Golan Heights in the distance, it stands in a picturesque setting of trees, gardens and fountains. Individuals can be seen in quiet meditation beside a cheerful fountain or beneath a climbing bougainvillea covered in colour. Groups are scattered throughout the grounds studying the Scriptures, addressing their spiritual quests in this human-made atmosphere of peace.

The church itself may appear to be a disruption to the serenity of its setting but it shows Jesus' message in a very visual manner.

'And yes,' Sarah was now the consummate tour guide holding the attention of her group, 'Antonio Barluzzi was the architect who designed this chapel, in case someone had in mind to ask me. It was built during 1936-38. It has also been said that the Italian dictator, Mussolini, contributed towards its construction.'

'How on earth did they know to build it here on top of this hill?' Margaret wanted to know. 'There are plenty of other hills around and Jesus would have probably climbed up them all. It doesn't say in the Bible where Jesus preached his sermon about the beatitudes — eight or nine or however many.'

A ripple of anticipation went through the group. Several smiles appeared as faces turned towards Margaret. Sarah ignored this knowing exactly that Margaret was still wanting to resurrect the discussion with Pastor Paul. 'No, Margaret, we cannot be absolutely sure that this was the place. However, we do have a record from the late fourth century, written by a pilgrim, a woman actually, who said Christians were already then commemorating the Sermon on the Mount on this hill. There was a Byzantine church built here around the same time. This present church is built very near the ruins of that old church.'

'We have to rely on tradition, then?' Colin suggested.

Sarah did not continue the discussion about sites and tradition but directed her listeners back to the church. 'If you look up you can see that this is built in the shape of an octagon; eight sided. On each of those frosted glass windows up there is written one of the beatitudes. Yes, it is in Latin. See that one there? **beati misericordes quia ipsi misericordiam consequentut.** Forgive my Latin pronunciation, but can anyone guess what that might mean?'

'That's the one about mercy or compassion,' someone suggested.

Then Avril recited, 'Blessed are the merciful, for they will be shown mercy.'

'That's right, Avril,' praised her friend Margaret. 'Remember we had to learn them all off by heart. But why did someone say compassion? It is mercy.'

Phillip's wife, Kaye, spoke up, 'I know most say mercy, but surely compassion is what Jesus was getting at. That's a more positive way for people to act. It's something we should be doing all the time. Mercy to me, has the idea that someone has to do something wrong to me before I can show mercy, whereas compassion is something I should be practising all the time.'

'It doesn't matter what we might think,' came back Avril, 'the Bible does say mercy. That is what I learnt.'

'And,' interrupted Sarah, seeing where the discussion could be heading, and not wanting another argument, 'make sure you have a good look at the symbols on the floor around the altar. They represent the traditional seven virtues. You know, justice, love, temperance, and so on.'

'Did you say traditional?' came a comment from Tony.

'Keep quiet, can't you?' Andrew spoke quickly, and he pulled his friend towards the side.

## Chapter 18  Beatitudes

The group gradually dispersed with Tony and Andrew walking around the colonnades which surrounded the church. Then Andrew left his friend, saying he wanted to spend some time alone in the garden area. He found a shady seat and was happy to sit for a while, looking out over the Sea of Galilee.

But not for long because after a few minutes Sarah sat down beside him.

'Hi,' she said.

'Oh, hello. How did you find me here?' replied Andrew.

'Actually, I wasn't really looking for you. I knew about this seat and felt like sitting down for a while. This is a great group of people, but I nearly had a few arguments back there.'

'Yes, I agree; but you handled it very well. Blessed are the peacemakers!'

'Nice one,' smiled Sarah. 'Say, if you are interested, we could have a quick look at the ruins of the old Byzantine church. Just a very short walk from here.'

'I'd like that,' agreed Andrew.

They got up and were walking side by side along a rough path when Sarah stumbled slightly. Andrew, who was speaking and looking towards her, quickly grabbed hold of her arm. Sarah regained her balance.

Andrew kept hold of her arm and continued walking. After a few steps he let go but Sarah took his hand in hers. She looked at him and smiled with an ever-so-slight blush appearing on her cheeks. Andrew gave her hand a gentle squeeze but did not let go. They continued making their way hand in hand.

Sarah stopped. 'Should I be doing this?' she queried.

'Should I be doing this?' Andrew replied.

They looked at one another, laughed and almost as one asked, 'Should we be doing this?'

Feed my sheep (John 21:17). Statue beside the lakeside Church of the Primacy of St Peter.

# Chapter 19

# Simon Peter

GALILEE, CIRCA 36 CE:

The Galilean preacher and teacher, Jesus, had been crucified by the Romans. He had died virtually alone, a condemned criminal, deserted by friends and followers. Even his closest disciples had fled when the Roman soldiers had come to arrest him.

His chosen disciples, Galileans all, had returned to the green hills of home, to their wives and children and to the peaceful waters of their lake. They were pleased to have escaped Jerusalem and its governing powers with their lives. They were back among the familiar faces in Galilee, but things were not the same; their minds were often back in Jerusalem or with their teacher and friend Jesus.

Life had to continue. There was no purpose in their sitting around discussing what might have been, how they might have stopped their master from going up to Jerusalem, what they might have done when they were in the Holy City. He was the master. He was driven by some power they did not really understand, and they just tagged along. Time moved on but their terrifying experience at the Passover festival remained. Their friend Jesus had been executed but would not go away.

Simon's wife and children could not see the old devil-may-care person in the man who had returned from that fateful Passover visit to Jerusalem. She tried to accept the change but found it hard to understand.

'You seem to be in a different world half the time,' she would say to him. 'What is going on?'

Simon would shake his head and reply, 'It's something that is happening time and time again. I can see him standing in front of me and he is asking, "Simon, do you still love me, or have you forgotten about me? Remember our times together, our discussions? How you agreed that I had something special to offer our people?" It just won't go away. How can I escape this?'

'What a strange thing for you to experience. And do you answer him when you feel him talking to you?' Simon's wife wanted to know.

'It depends. Often not, but sometimes his presence is so real. I feel changed inside and at these times, yes, I must admit I do reply and say that I haven't forgotten him and that I still do love him.'

Weeks turned into months and Jesus' disciples quickly slipped back into the routine they had followed since beginning their jobs on the fishing boats. They knew it so well: trolling the depths of the Sea of Galilee during the night and heading back to shore with their catch at daybreak.

One such occasion was nearing its end. The sky was beginning to brighten in the east and the tired fishermen in the boat could faintly make out the bulk of the Decapolis mountain block. The water however was still dark and uninviting. On the surface there was but a dim reflection of the faint fat-lamp on the bow of the boat.

'Another absolute waste of time,' said Thomas. 'You know, Simon, I didn't really think we were ever in the right spot. We should have been further over towards Gergesa.'

'Now you tell me,' replied Simon. 'If you were so sure why didn't you say something before, while we were out there breaking our backs for nothing?'

'Well, I wasn't absolutely sure. I just had the feeling. Had there been a little moonlight... '

James and John had been listening to the conversation and decided to interrupt before it got too heated. They knew how Simon would lose his patience with Thomas who was a bit of a ditherer and could never come to any conclusion.

'Maybe our Lord God didn't want us to catch anything tonight,' suggested James. 'Our dad believes that God sometimes wants to show us who is really in charge of the wind, water and fish.'

'Yes,' said Thomas, 'there are a lot of folk around here who agree with old Zebedee.' Then turning to Simon, James said, 'You know, Simon, since we've come back to the boats after Jesus was executed, you don't seem to be fully with it.'

'I agree,' said young John. 'We agreed to get back on the boats, but I think it was mainly your idea. You thought that it would take our minds away from those days up in Jerusalem. But it doesn't seem to have worked. Things just aren't like they used to be.'

'You're right,' Simon said. 'I'm sorry. I can't seem to concentrate on what I should be doing. The Master seems to be with me whatever I do. My mind is often thousands of miles away.'

'Doesn't that frustrate you?' Thomas asked.

'Well, yes, but then again not really,' Simon admitted. 'That's just the point. During those times when I feel that the Master is with me, my life seems so purposeful. I seem to be experiencing something new. He seems to be standing next to me and yet he's not. Does that make any sense? Have any of you ever felt like that?'

In the brightening darkness each member of the small group of friends on board the boat could sense the scrutiny of others. For some time, nothing could be heard except the lapping of the water on the sides of the boat.

James spoke and broke the tension. 'I think I know what you

mean. A feeling has come over me at times when I think time has stood still. I feel a new power. It is as though God and Galilee have come together in me. Then I have a strange urge wanting to tell other people how I feel.'

'How you feel about what, or about whom?'

'The Master of course. And then I end up asking myself if this is really God speaking to us?'

Simon took up this idea. 'That's not a silly question. Is God telling us that Jesus was someone so special that he would not let us forget him? Just because his enemies killed him did not mean the end, rather the beginning.'

'How are those nets?'

'What do you expect? Just some sticks and sea grass. I've had enough of this.'

'The Master always wanted us to be different. Let's have one more try. But to be different we'll put the net down on the other side of the boat. We will keep rowing to the shore and see if anyone else has had any luck.'

The next half hour saw each man in the boat doing what he had been trained to do as a child. Working in unison the crew lowered the empty net on, to their way of thinking, the wrong side of the boat. The men on the oars strained and the boat moved slowly forward.

'What the'… exclaimed Nathanael working the front oar. 'We've snagged something. Whose bright idea was it to put the net over in this shallow water?'

Simon and John were pulling at the net trying to gauge where the trouble lay. Suddenly, Simon gave a shout and jumped into the water, tripped and fell headlong. When his head emerged from under the waves he shouted out, 'Pull! Pull! But be careful. You won't believe this, but the net is full of bloody, great fish!'

## Chapter 19   Simon Peter

The Church of the Beatitudes had been the first stop for the day. Then followed visits to other churches in this neighbourhood. The last few hours of the tour had left a blur of buildings in many minds and a compendium of comments spinning around in others. The whole morning had been rushed and the weather did not help brighten the mood of the people. It was very hot. They were now slowly walking down a tree-lined avenue, including a number of fine, tall eucalypts, when Colin said to no one in particular, 'I'm just about churched out. What's this one all about?'

It was indeed a fact that the last few hours had been a case of 'in the bus', a very short drive, 'out of the bus', 'forty minutes should be enough', a quick visit to the church, 'which church?', 'is everyone back yet?' a short drive...

Sitting for a while in the shade of the cooling eucalypts was a welcome prospect. Some took the opportunity while others pressed on. They were approaching a chunky, blue-stone chapel with the blue waters of the Sea of Galilee shining behind it. A small, rectangular sign near the front entrance reading *Sacellum Primatus Sancti Petri* provided an answer to those who were wondering which church they were now visiting. The sign would provide an answer, assuming that some basic school Latin had not been forgotten.

Phillip looked at the sign and then turned to his wife. 'Who learns Latin at school these days?'

'We should be able to work it out,' suggested Kaye. 'I can see St Peter there but what about those first two words, *Sacellum Primatus?*'

Pastor Paul came to the rescue. 'This is the chapel of the Primacy of St Peter.'

'The Primacy of St Peter? That's still Latin to me, or should I say it's now Greek to me?' said Phillip. 'What's it really all about?'

Pastor Paul resisted saying that Phillip should read chapter

21 in John and he would then know all about it. He realised that this chapter has always seemed a little strange, being apparently tacked on to the end of a book that seemed to be finished at the end of chapter 20. For many it raises as many questions as it answers. But that was another matter which would be of little interest to Phillip.

Instead he said, 'This chapel commemorates events that are related in a few verses in John chapter 21. Wait a minute.'

With that he took out his iPad from his shoulder bag, quickly got into his e-Bible and read from John 21: 15-17:

> When they had finished eating, Jesus said to Simon Peter, "Simon, son of John, do you love me more than these?"
>
> "Yes, Lord," he said, "you know that I love you."
>
> Jesus said, "Feed my lambs."
>
> Again, Jesus said, "Simon, son of John, do you truly love me?"
>
> He answered, "Yes, Lord, you know that I love you."
>
> Jesus said, "Take care of my sheep."
>
> The third time he said to him, "Simon, son of John, do you love me?"
>
> Peter was hurt because Jesus asked him a third time, "Do you love me?" He said, "Lord, you know all things; you know that I love you."
>
> Jesus said, "Feed my sheep."

'Fine,' said Phillip, 'but what's that got to do with the primacy of St Peter? What you have read is merely soliciting a response from Peter which would encourage him to carry on spreading Jesus' message of love.'

It was evident that Pastor Paul had been asked something similar before for he had his answer ready. 'True, it does that, but one can read much more into those sentences. Keeping in mind Peter's thrice denial at the crucifixion, this three times questioning of his love towards his Lord is taken as Jesus reinstating Peter as the leader of the apostles. Jesus' final reply of "Feed my sheep" implies that he should now dedicate his life to proclaiming the Gospel; a compelling invitation from Jesus.'

Phillip accepted this explanation, rather reluctantly, if the frown on his face had any significance.

The bronze statue, on the shore of the Sea near the chapel is a graphic picture of Jesus "knighting" Peter for his future job, with the shepherd's crook. The chapel and the nearby statue commemorate the site where, according to tradition, Jesus' forgiveness of Peter was forthcoming. Whether it is or it isn't, is not really that important. What is important is the story told by John and physically represented here has had so many repercussions in the centuries since then.

As with many of the holy sites in Israel, this church is administered by the Franciscan Custody of the Holy Land. It is relatively new, being built in 1933. However, as is the case with many other churches in the country, it was built on the foundations of a much earlier church dating back to the fourth century.

Inside the church one finds a memorial to another of the events related in John, chapter 21. This concerns Jesus cooking a breakfast of fish for the seven disciples who were present on this occasion. The fish came from a bountiful catch which the fishermen-disciples had just made at the suggestion of Jesus. The limestone rock pushing up through the floor of the chapel in front of the altar is reputed to be the "table" on which Jesus prepared and served this breakfast. It is known as the *Mensa Christi* (table of Christ), as the adjacent sign there indicates.

The tables and seats in the shade of the many trees around the chapel were beckoning. Some of the group had decided not to go wading in the rocky waters of the Sea of Galilee here and had already stretched themselves out on the seats. Soon the others had joined them. Tired limbs and overtaxed minds were now crying out for everyone to remain and rest but a stronger force was reminding them of their next stop. The morning had flown so quickly, it was already one thirty and hunger was calling.

It was Gordon who called for attention. 'We're running a bit late and I know you must be hungry. We are going to a special restaurant for lunch and I'm sure you will agree later that the waiting was worth it.'

'Are you shouting, Gordon?'

Gordon smiled. 'That had crossed my mind. But no, I'm sorry, not this time.'

'So when is the next time?'

Gordon ignored the question and merely said, 'We have to move back to the bus now. It won't be a long drive. Just a few minutes. During that time Margaret will read a short passage from the Bible. You will be able to see its relevance when we arrive at the restaurant.'

In the bus Margaret began reading from the Gospel of Matthew:

> *When they had come to Capernaum, those who received the temple tax came to Peter and said, "Does your teacher not pay the temple tax?" He said, "Yes." And when he had come into the house, Jesus anticipated him saying, "What do you think, Simon? From whom do kings of the earth take customs or taxes, from their sons or from strangers?" Peter said to him, "From strangers." Jesus said to him, "Then the sons are free. Nevertheless, lest we offend them, go to the sea, cast in a hook, and take the fish that comes up first. And when you*

have opened its mouth, you will find a piece of money; take that and give it to them for Me and you."

The reading had barely finished when they pulled into a crowded car park. Their destination? It was St Peter's Restaurant, a large glass-fronted building looking out over the Sea of Galilee. The group was scheduled to have lunch of fish and chips.

Actually, that's probably putting it a little mundanely. It was really going to be a special meal consisting of the type of fish which grew out of the last sentences of the passage Margaret had just read — *take the fish that comes up first. And when you have opened its mouth, you will find a piece of money.* According to tradition, Peter following Jesus' suggestion, had caught a Tilapia, one of the fish most caught by the fishermen of that time. It became known as the St Peter's fish. A hospitality industry has grown up here on the shores of the Sea of Galilee catering to the visitors who are happy to spend their hard-earned drachmas to eat this fish and meditate on the great fisherman himself. This was possibly the case for some, but for others, more probably just to have a good meal and taste the fish.

While they were waiting for the chef to cook their sample of biblical tradition, Tony leant over to Margaret and Avril who were sitting opposite him and said, 'I must tell you about an acquaintance of mine. Some years ago, he was starting up an aquaculture business. I was surprised and told him so.'

'Yes, and?' Margaret showed her interest.

'Then I asked him what prompted him to go into that sort of business. And do you know what he said?'

'No,' said Margaret. 'Perhaps, mind your own business.'

Tony smiled and shook his head. 'No, he told me that there's money in fish.'

Phillip and Kaye who were also sitting opposite Tony laughed. Margaret and Avril looked at one another with a puzzled look.

Their orders had arrived by now and there was quietness around the table for everyone was very hungry. Margaret and Avril had chosen the whole fish with rice and Tony and Andrew opted for the filleted version with salad and chips.

'You know something,' began Tony when he had finished eating.

Avril looked up. 'Well, what now?'

'Just look around at all these people here eating fish and chips. I bet Matthew when he wrote that bit which Margaret read on the bus, had no idea what a profitable business would develop because of him.'

'What do you mean?'

'Well, it's hard to beat a good feed of fish and chips. Yes, there sure is money in fish.'

\* \* \* \*

### Extract from Andrew's travel diary:

We had come from the Mount of the Beatitudes on the Galilee Sea to Mt Bental in the Golan Heights. No, we hadn't moved along the alphabet very far! We did travel, however, from "Blessed are the peacemakers for they shall be called the children of God", to the United Nations peacekeepers for they are needed here. One short, uphill drive had traversed millennia of history as well as a broad spectrum of human experiences.

A gap had appeared in our very tight travel schedule and Sarah, our never-one-to-sit-still guide, had suggested the possibility of driving to the Golan Heights, not describing specifically what might be seen there. The name itself prompted a

## Chapter 19  Simon Peter

unanimous decision to have Masoud drive us there. The older members of the group seemed aware of the significance of the name, whereas for others the name meant nothing.

We wound our way up the old volcano of Mt Bental hoping that Masoud would keep his eyes, and the bus as well, on the narrow road. We arrived at the summit wondering what exactly we would find to interest us. There was first a few Druze farmers inviting us to taste their fruit. Many did. I did and found it very good indeed! Then we walked through a short avenue of quaint iron sculptures, pieces of art created by Dutch artist, Joop de Jong. Quaint and humorous, one must agree, but I did hear a few of our party debating whether **art** accurately described the works. It is one way to recycle old rusty iron.

And then the summit and the peacekeepers. There were two blue-bereted soldiers, representatives of the UN peacekeeping force stationed here, high overlooking the no-go zone between Israel and Syria. These two service personnel, one from The Netherlands and one from New Zealand, smiled a welcome to us visitors. Bless them, for at any time the boredom of their watch could change to the danger of being in the path of conflicting armies. As it was, the dullness of their watch today was brightened by lively conversation and questioning from interested members of our group.

The peacefulness of this outpost belies the horror of the conflict raging in Syria not so many kilometres away. The sounds of war are heard in the quiet of an approaching evening. Conflict, recognised by a dull thud, by a reverberating boom, reaches our ears. These are the sounds of exploding anger. To us it is only distant noise, albeit noise with meaning, but to those whose houses are destroyed, whose livelihoods are shattered, whose eardrums are burst, whose lives are sacrificed, what is it to them? I shall never understand.

The empty trenches here on this mount, the silhouetted tin soldiers, the silent guns, stand as a memorial to a conflict almost half a century ago. This war, known as the Yom Kippur War, began on the Jewish holy day of Yom Kippur in 1973. On this day armies from various Arab countries surrounding Israel launched attacks, across the Sinai in the south and on the Golan Height in the north. Here on Mt Bental the monument remembers especially the battle against overwhelming Syrian forces. These initially made advances but were later driven back. The result was burnt out tanks littering the landscape and soldiers lying dead and dying. A continuing conflict.

Put in perspective, however, I suppose this site commemorates just one of the bloody conflicts which litter the pages of any Israeli history book. Open the history books of the Old Testament and one finds Ammonites and Amorites, Philistines and Palestines, Hittites and Edomites all in conflict with the Israelites. Not to mention the Assyrians and Babylonians and Egyptians.

As is the case with all battles — those remembered such as Waterloo, Anzac Cove, Leningrad, (the list is long), and those not remembered, (this list is probably longer) — many are sacrificed, few are benefitted. I shall never understand.

## Chapter 20

# Yom Kippur

It was quiet on the waterfront; no boat was moving. The shouts and chatter of the fishermen preparing for another day of work out on the water could not be heard. Their boats remained unmanned and their nets uncast. Even the water seemed all but becalmed. The sea was quiet, merely gently lapping its rocky shores. Across the glassy waters of the Sea of Galilee no vessel was to be seen. All was peaceful.

The rough timber stalls in the market place adjoining the port area were closed; locked up firmly, left to stand alone. The area around McDonald's was deserted, the doors closed. The golden arches were abandoned, well, temporarily. The car park stood vacant; no vehicle was to be seen. Just a solitary cyclist was slowly peddling down the street. The wheels of the tourists' busses were not turning, hastening to the next holy site. The roads would feel easier, having the weight which they usually had to bear lifted from their shoulders. It was as though the town had been forsaken.

But it was not forsaken, merely responding to the Jewish holiday of Yom Kippur. Here in Tiberius, as in all of Israel, it was 10 Tishrei (the tenth day of the seventh month). This was Yom Kippur. Today was the day the land of Israel stood still. Twenty-four hours to nowhere. Peace and quiet was to reign. The people take time to meditate, to reflect, to repent and ask God to forgive their many trespasses. At the end of the day the people will feel easier, having the weight of their trespasses lifted from their shoulders.

As a physical act of repentance, a sevenfold washing in water is often carried out. As they purify themselves by this sevenfold washing in water, here in Tiberius in the sweet waters of the Sea of Galilee, so may God wash them clean of their sins. The celebration of this holy day is in accordance with their Scriptures where, in the Book of Leviticus, chapter16, verse 29, it is written:

> *This is to be a lasting ordinance for you: on the tenth day of the seventh month you must deny yourselves and not do any work — whether native-born or an alien living among you — for on this day atonement will be made for you, to cleanse you. Then before the Lord you will be free from all your sins. It is a Sabbath of rest and you must deny yourselves; it is a lasting ordinance.*

At the end of what for many Israelis is an emotional 24 hours, they hope that this greeting will ring true: *gmar chatimah tova* (that you will finish with a good stamp in God's book).

Sarah had elected to undergo the sevenfold immersion in the Sea of Galilee as a ritual for this holy day. She was joined by a small number of Gordon's touring party who chose also to be part of the Yom Kippur ceremony of repentance and atonement. Other members of the group stood on the shore or in the shallow water and watched the going under and re-emerging of those out further in the deeper water.

Arrangements had been made to visit a local synagogue later in the morning and until then sitting at the tables around the pool was the choice of many. The excitement and expectation of what was coming up next on the itinerary, the main topics of conversation early in the tour, had now given way to reflecting on and discussing what had already been experienced. One group was happily cataloguing and assessing the many gifts and souvenirs which had already been purchased. The six heads at a nearby, less noisy table were closely following their fingers on the iPads or mobiles making sure nothing was missed on Facebook.

Relationships among members of the group had generally remained very cordial, a testimony to the professionalism of tour leader, Gordon, guide Sarah and Pastor Paul. Inevitably there would always be a few hiccups along the way; slight disagreements. It was also common for certain regular groups to establish whose members had sensed some form of affinity with one another. It didn't surprise Margaret and Avril who were sitting talking to Colin and Emma when Tony and Andrew sat down on the two vacant chairs at their table.

Andrew looked at Margaret and Avril and then said, 'Didn't see you two out there being ducked this morning. Too cold for you?'

'No,' replied Avril, 'that was a Jewish thing and as Christians there was no reason for us to be involved. What about you two? You didn't go out either, did you?'

'Fair enough,' agreed Andrew. 'No, we just watched from the shore.'

'Yes,' came in Margaret, 'we saw you staring at our tour guide as she was wading out.'

'Can't blame us, can you?' said Tony. 'After all, we are just two normal young fellows.'

'Anyway,' interrupted Colin, 'we were just discussing which sites impressed us most so far. Tell us Tony, what site held most significance for you?'

'Just let me think,' replied Tony. 'I would say the Church of the Beatitudes.'

'What?' the two women said in unison, somewhat surprised at the choice. 'The Church of the Beatitudes. Why on earth that one?'

'That's the one down beside the water, isn't it?' stated Avril.

'No, Avril,' came in Margaret immediately. 'You're thinking of the Church of the Primacy of St Peter. That's the one down near the shore. The Beatitudes one is up on the hill overlooking the Sea of Galilee.'

'Oh, dear, that's right. We've seen so many churches that I'm becoming confused.'

'Don't worry,' consoled her friend. 'I think we are all getting a little tired of seeing all these different churches. But, Tony, why did you like that church up there on the hill?'

Tony had his answer all ready. 'It illustrates to me what Christian faith is all about.'

'How does it show that?' Colin wanted to know.

Tony explained. 'It's not the site, beautiful as it may be. Or the flash building with its symbolism. I see being a Christian as putting myself in the hands of God, the God which is known through Jesus. Jesus' Sermon on the Mount, which the church commemorates, is a good wrap-up of what the Christian life is all about.'

Emma was nodding in agreement. 'All makes sense to me,' she said. 'What about you Margaret? Which is your favourite place so far?'

'Both Avril and I would agree that it would have to be Bethlehem,' she replied.

'Bethlehem?' This time the boys seemed surprised and Tony continued, 'What? That old church? Bumping your head to get into it. Then hearing about the squabbles between the Catholics, the Armenians and the Greeks as to who has a right to be there. Then that star down in the cave.' He stopped, wondering what to say next.

'It was an experience all right,' he then added.

## Chapter 20  Yom Kippur

'If you just give me a chance I'll tell you why Bethlehem was important to me,' Margaret insisted.

'Good idea,' said Colin. You two be quiet for a while and let the ladies speak. Avril... '

'Well it was Bethlehem where Jesus was born. Without Bethlehem there would be no Jesus and where would that leave us all? And then... '

'But Avril,' interrupted both Tony and Andrew at the same time. They looked at one another and then Andrew continued, 'Does it really matter where Jesus was born? Mark wasn't interested in where he was born when he wrote his Gospel. Nor was John. Neither was Paul in all his epistles. It was only Matthew and then Luke who came up with the idea that he was born in Bethlehem.'

The Tony broke in. 'Isn't it enough to know that he was born somewhere and existed? And there's no argument there.'

'No,' said Avril. 'I was brought up to believe that everything in the Bible is correct. And that's all there is to it. Why is it that every time Margaret and I start talking to you two that we end up having an argument?'

'Not really an argument, Avril,' suggested Tony. 'It's just a different way of looking at things. And do you know what? I think you two just love discussing things with us.'

At this point they watched as Gordon came up to their table, and they knew what he was going to say. Before he could say anything, Colin spoke up, 'Gordon, you seem to have a knack of coming and interrupting us just as we are in the middle of a deep discussion. Well, probably not so deep this time.'

'Sorry, people. I hope it wasn't too heated.'

'No,' said Andrew. 'The ladies were just agreeing that Tony and I are fine young fellows.'

Gordon smiled. 'I find that hard to believe. But I've come to tell you that we will be moving off down to the synagogue in ten minutes. That is if you plan to come along. I want to give you time to get yourselves organised.,

Avril looked questioningly at Margaret which made Gordon continue, 'No, only if you want to come. Some are staying back here at the hotel and resting.'

A short time later, Gordon and Sarah were leading a smaller group, many decked out in their Persil whites, along Tiberius' deserted streets to one of the synagogues located in the city. This one was in the old city area, a short walking distance from the hotel. They were walking along a street paved in small, square, black basalt pavers when Sarah called a halt. They had arrived at their destination.

All were surprised. They had visited many religious buildings on their pilgrimage to date and all had been imposing, standing out as something special. Here, however, behind a high, black fence with mildly ornate gates stood a very unimposing building squashed between two much larger structures.

Can this be to where they were headed? To non-Jewish eyes, unable to read the sign on the front wall of the building, there seemed to be no visible evidence that this was a house of worship. The two Stars of David depicted on the main sign did indicate that this building was something specifically Jewish. Sarah saw the concern in some of the eyes and she commented, 'Yes, this is the synagogue. What were you expecting? The temple of Solomon?'

A couple of men were talking in the small, front courtyard which was completely paved over with light-coloured bricks. There was no green, no vegetation to soften the stark appearance. Two other men sat slouched on dull, grey plastic chairs. The building was two storied with the top floor sitting uncomfortably on its lower support, architecturally somewhat jarring. The

## Chapter 20  Yom Kippur

lower wall was constructed of building blocks of varying colours whereas the upper floor was evenly plastered in a dun colour. This flat, rectangular surface was broken by two slightly ornate windows. These two windows, as well as the dome-shaped one in the lower area were protected by black bars.

An exterior staircase on the left-hand edge of the building gave access to the upper floor. Sarah directed the women in the party to these stairs whereas the men entered via the front ground floor door. The fine black iron mesh which formed the railing of the staircase acted as a modesty panel so that the women mounting the stairs would not be embarrassed.

Surprise awaited everyone on entering this building.

\* \* \*

**EXTRACT FROM ANDREW'S TRAVEL DIARY:**

Looking forward to Yom Kippur today for I was gradually becoming more and more tired; or should I say quickly and not gradually! Put on my white shirt (brought especially as per instructions in our tour package) and light-coloured trousers as a sign of solidarity with those whose land I was visiting. It is the Jewish custom to wear white on this day (wash them and they shall be as white as snow). My action is a sign of respect for their religion. Most of the group did this as well. Together we might have been mistaken for an Aussie XI after a hard day in the field.

Sarah apparently had arranged that Pastor Paul would officiate at her sevenfold immersion in the Sea of Galilee; a meeting of the Jewish and Christian faiths. They made quite a sight wading into the lake, he in his white gown and she in a white bathing costume. It was a two-piece costume.

It struck me once again just how attractive Sarah is. Sure, I had agreed with Tony that she was "a good-looking sort" (his words) but seeing her move into the water made my heart sort of jump. It's ironic looking back at the situation. Here was Sarah, a good Jewess, on one of her most holy days, totally reflecting on her relationship with God, and there I stood, probably a little ashamed to say, thinking about things a little more physical and basic. But how wrong can it be to look at a woman and feel her beauty affecting you? Did she realise the effect her ceremony was having on me? I'm sure not!

Tony and I were standing together watching Pastor Paul and her enter the water and again when she returned to shore, smiling and laughing, clearly responding to the freedom she felt after receiving God's forgiveness. Tony looked at me watching her. I saw him smile, but he made no comment. That surprised me, however there will be plenty made in the future, no doubt.

I wonder will I ever get the chance, or will it ever be appropriate, to tell her how attractive I think she is? The bad news is that I have only five days to win Sarah's favour. But I suppose on the other hand the good news is that I do have five days to win her favour. Should I really be writing this?

## Chapter 21

# In the Synagogue

Joseph, the local synagogue attendant was so very highly elated to be able to take his visitors on a tour of his special place. All the visitors on their part were so thankful for the opportunity offered and showed devout attention to all his explanations.

On entering the building many looked around to locate the Holy Scroll for that was something they understood to be in a synagogue. There were plenty of books, large and small, on display in the room but no obvious scrolls. When asked, Joseph agreed to show the Holy Scroll and he went to a richly-embellished wallhanging. He drew back the curtain, unlocked the wooden doors, slid aside another layer of doors to expose beautiful, shining silver containers. He opened one of these for all to see a scroll with clear black writing on brilliant white paper.

Everyone felt privileged to have the opportunity to see a little further into the Jewish religion.

Located on another wall was a list of Jewish festival days: Shavuot, Rosh Hashanah, Yom Kippur, etc. and Purim. Andrew innocently asked the significance of Purim which prompted an immediate response in which Guide Sarah, Pastor Paul and the synagogue official Joseph, all participated.

Joseph was impressed by the contributions of the other two. What manner of tour guide is this, he thought, who is so sincere and knowledgeable about our blessed religion? And what manner of Christian pastor is this whose knowledge of our religious text far exceeds that of most others who come here to visit. And what manner of a pilgrim group is this which is content to stand and listen to us relating all ten chapters of the Book of Esther?

It is the Old Testament book of Esther which is the basis of the Jewish festival day of Purim. The tale told by the three impromptu storytellers lacked the continuity and Biblical phraseology found in most versions of the Bible but it held the attention of the group gathered around. Several other visitors who happened to enter the area moved over to the group to listen in.

Their version ran basically as follows:

The powerful King Xerxes ruled his Persian Empire, which stretched from India to Ethiopia, from his citadel of Susa. He was one for throwing parties to show off his wealth and liberality. At one such party, after having imbibed a little too liberally he ordered his eunuchs to bring his wife, Queen Vashti, to the banquet. She was an acclaimed beauty and the King wanted to show her off in front of his guests.

But the queen refused to come.

The mighty king was furious. This could not be tolerated or soon all the wives in the Empire would be disobeying their husbands. He immediately sent an edict throughout all of his 127 provinces that every man should be ruler over his own household.

Now what to do with Queen Vashti? His advisers suggested that he divorce her and begin a search for a beautiful, young virgin who would become his new queen. King Xerxes was in agreement and finally chose a young girl, Esther, whom he installed in the palace.

Esther was an orphaned Jewish girl who was being raised by her cousin, Mordecai. The King had not been informed that Esther was Jewish. After Esther had been taken to the palace Mordecai missed her dreadfully for she had been like a daughter to him, and every day he walked up and down near the palace to be near her. One day he overheard how two of the King's officers were planning to assassinate their ruler. Mordecai reported what he had heard to Queen Esther who passed the information on to the king, but giving credit to Mordecai.

The officers were apprehended, duly punished, and Mordecai's name was recorded in the *Book of Friends of the King*.

The episode caused a reorganisation of the King's administration and a man named Haman was elected to a position next in power to the King. Unfortunately, power went to Haman's head and he decreed that everyone should bow down and pay homage to him. Mordecai refused to do this. Haman was enraged and when he realised that Mordecai was a Jew he was determined to destroy not only this man who refused to honour him, but all the Jews in the Empire.

Haman and his henchmen cast the *pur* (that is they cast lots) to determine on which day the purge would take place. The thirteenth day of the month of Adar was selected. Haman then issued orders under the seal of the King's signet ring and couriers were sent to all the provinces of the Empire.

Mordecai, the Jew, was very alarmed when he learnt what was about to happen. He approached Queen Esther suggesting that she should beg the King for help. Naturally she agreed to do what she could to help her Jewish people. She sought an audience with the King realising full well the danger in which she was placing herself. Because of his great love for her, the King agreed to listen to her request.

Esther asked that the King and Haman come to a private banquet which she was organising. Her request at this first banquet was that the King and Haman come to a second banquet when she would make known her real request.

Haman was beside himself with pride. He boasted to all how he alone had been invited to dine with the Queen and King. His followers were also happy, and all bowed down to pay him respect. But not Mordecai, the Jew. This enraged Haman and he had a gallows erected on which to hang this pesky Jew.

In the meantime, King Xerxes, during a sleepless evening, while browsing through his *Book of Friends of the King*, came across Mordecai's name and wondered how he had been honoured for what he had done. His servants informed him that Mordecai had received nothing. The King, determined to redress this oversight, asked Haman what should be done to someone who had performed a deed that saved the King's life. Thinking that the King was speaking about him, Haman gave a long list of honours that this man should receive. Haman was then told to go and give these honours to Mordecai, the Jew, who was always walking up and down in front of the palace.

Oh, the disbelief, but Haman did as he was told. He was a worried man. His friends agreed that he was in trouble.

Worse was to follow for Haman.

That night at the second banquet, the King asked Esther for her request and she begged that her people be spared from annihilation. The King was furious and wanted to know who was planning this heinous deed. Esther pointed to Haman. The King was further enraged and had him hanged on the gallows which he had built for Mordecai. He immediately revoked the edict ordering the massacre of the Jews, confiscated Haman's property and gave it to Esther. Mordecai was now elevated to a high position.

There followed great celebrations in the Jewish communities throughout the land. Mordecai decreed that this day of rejoicing and feasting be celebrated annually. People were to remember that this was a time when the Jews got relief from their enemies.

So was born the festival of Purim.

After the lengthy Holy Scroll recitation everyone was pleased to be able to move around again inspecting the various details

## Chapter 21  In the Synagogue

inside the synagogue. It was a relaxed atmosphere for no official worship service was taking place. Several men carefully reading books open on the table before them merely gave the visitors a casual glance. Another small group was engaged in light-hearted talk. They gave the intruders a friendly smile and continued with their conversation.

On this festive day of Yom Kippur, the Christian pilgrims had become more acquainted with not one, but two, Jewish festivals.

Around the dinner table that evening, the twenty-four-hour celebration of Yom Kippur now over, the conversation was mostly about the two Jewish festivals which had been experienced that day.

'You know, Pastor,' said Colin, 'what made today especially interesting was the fact that we were experiencing non-Christian things.'

'Oh,' responded a non-committal Pastor Paul. Others at the table looked at Colin waiting for further information.

'Well, put it like this,' explained Colin. 'We go to... let's say, the Shepherds' Field, an interesting little chapel, sure, but we all know the story. Many of us know it by heart. Or the Chapel of the Beatitudes. Again, we all know the story, the details. Yes, and some of us could recite the beatitudes by heart. Today we were on unknown territory. I think that made it more interesting.'

'I agree,' said Tony. 'Talking about Purim. I know that the book of Esther is in the Old Testament. I may have read it at some time, but I don't really remember. So I really learnt something today.'

'Now I see what you are getting at,' said Pastor Paul. 'Yes, it is good to broaden one's knowledge about other religions. And no, one doesn't hear much about the Book of Esther in our Lutheran churches.'

'It's a good story, but why do we have it in the Bible?' asked Andrew.

'But, it's in the Bible, so you can't question it,' Avril made her opinion known.

Tony took up Andrew's point. 'Tell me, Avril, what's it got to do with Christianity?'

'Hold off, Tony,' interrupted Pastor Paul. 'I don't think that's a very fair question. You can't expect to start a theological discussion at the drop of a hat.'

'I should have kept my mouth shut,' remarked Andrew.

'What do you mean, Andrew?'

'Well, it was I who asked what the festival of Purim was all about. It was just a simple question.'

'I think we all have learnt something from it,' consoled Pastor Paul. 'It is a fact that there are theologians who question whether the Book of Esther should be in the Canon. I believe that Martin Luther even queried why it should be there.'

'Any idea how Purim is actually celebrated?' asked Colin. 'I trust not like that mentioned in the Bible where the Jews started massacring their enemies.'

Tony was quick to find an answer. He called out to Sarah who was sitting a few tables away. 'Hey, Sarah, mind coming over her for a minute? We have a problem.'

'Sure,' replied Sarah, ever ready to help. She came over and Colin explained what they wanted.

'How we celebrate Purim,' repeated Sarah. 'Well it's not a particularly religious affair although, as you heard today, it has its roots in the Book of Esther and what is written there. Basically, it's a holiday when people party, eat a lot, often drink too much and exchange gifts.'

'There you are Avril,' said Tony after hearing Sarah's assessment of the holiday. 'Seems a good enough reason to have Esther in the Bible, don't you think?'

## Chapter 22

# Cana

Twenty kilometres west of the cool waters of the Sea of Galilee, in dry hill country, lies the town of Kfar Kana. Although hotly disputed by many biblical scholars, this town is identified with the Cana of John 2:1-11, where according to the Evangelist, Jesus attended a wedding and changed water into wine. This "miraculous sign" of Jesus, his first according to John's Gospel, is commemorated by the Franciscan Wedding Chapel located in the old section of the town.

This chapel is the focus of the pilgrims' visit to Cana. Many come here to meditate on the glory of Jesus and others to tick off another Jesus place they have visited. There are also many visitors who come here to take the opportunity of renewing their previous wedding vows in the main church or the smaller adjunct chapel; some indeed to be married for the first time.

As was normally the case, Tony and Andrew were among the first to board the bus which today was headed for the marriage city. They were greeted by Sarah with a welcoming smile on her lips and a bunch of red roses in her hand.

'Oh, you shouldn't have,' said Tony as a greeting.

'Shouldn't have what?' replied Sarah.

'Brought all those red roses along for me. I didn't realise you cared so much.'

Sarah blushed but quickly recovered. 'Sorry, Tony. They are for several other people. I didn't want to embarrass you with a red rose. You can have one of the balloons if you want to. Pick your own colour.'

Andrew spoke up before Tony could come back with some comment. 'Hello. Would it be OK if we sat in one of these front seats today? No one else has booked them, have they?'

'No,' replied Sarah. 'I'd love you to sit down here in the front. You have always been going to the back like two naughty school boys.'

'We promise to behave if you leave us sit here in the front,' promised Tony.

They sat down which allowed the others waiting behind them to come in. This morning the interior of the coach was decked out in celebratory garb. Balloons of various colours bobbed around buffeting the faces of the passengers as they moved along to find a seat. There were startled cries when the first balloon popped — or was popped — but fewer and fewer as the popping continued.

The excitement for many mounted as the bus made its way to the Cana wedding, or in this case the Cana weddings. Five couples had chosen to renew their marriage vows in the church built to remember the well-known story in John's Gospel. Pastor Paul had prepared an order of service appropriate to the situation. The ritual was celebrated with all the other members of the party looking on.

On the way out of the chapel, Andrew looked at Tony and asked, 'Well, what did you think of that?'

'I must say it was quite impressive. Mind you, I've never had any personal experience of being married but it's easy to see why those couples wanted to be part of it. And you?'

'Me? Yes, I agree with you. I have no doubt that the whole ceremony would have been especially memorable for the ten souls who were brave enough to be married once again.'

## Chapter 22  Cana

'Brave?' asked Tony.

'No, I'm joking. I'm sure it was wonderful for them to renew their marriage vows. Is that better? After all, as Pastor Paul said in his address, many do see John's story of the wedding at Cana as Jesus' affirmation of the sanctity of marriage. Receiving Jesus' blessing here on their reaffirmed union would feel especially apposite.'

'Stop! Stop! That's a better answer, but I don't want another sermon now.' Tony interrupted his friend who clearly had more to say on the matter.

But Andrew did continue. 'It was an interesting wedding ceremony, but I must admit that my mind wandered a bit during the proceedings.'

'Yes, I know what you mean,' said Tony. 'It happens to me all the time. There always seems to be some compelling power in my pew that tends to deflect my thoughts away from what the preacher is trying to emphasise. But I think I have a fair idea of what you were thinking about.'

'Don't be silly. How could you possibly know?' replied Andrew.

'Well,' went on Tony, 'a few times when I looked at you I saw your eyes "wandering" as you put it, over to Sarah standing near the doorway, and ... no, wait a minute and listen ... I'm sure I saw how her glances met yours.'

'Get away with you. You've always had a very vivid imagination. No, I wasn't dreaming of marrying Sarah, if that's what you were getting at. I was thinking of a discussion I had some time ago with my sister's husband who said that John was really writing about Jesus' own wedding.'

'What? That Jesus was married in Cana?'

'Yes, he maintained that on a careful, thoughtful reading of the text one would discover that no less a person than Jesus himself was the bridegroom there.'

'And what did you say?' asked Tony who seemed interested

in the way the conversation was headed. He was always ready to consider argumentative ideas when religion was being discussed.

'Well, I don't remember exactly, but I think I said something about how it was strange that he had to be invited to his own wedding.'

'So, you would say that a casual reading of John's story would show that Jesus was just a guest?'

'If you put it like that, yes,' agreed Andrew.

By this time the group had made its way to a nearby wine/souvenir shop where one of the newly reweds had organised a wedding cake and naturally, in keeping with the overall theme of the day and of Jesus' first miraculous sign, plenty of good wine.

Until a few decades ago, if one were to ask the general person in the street if Jesus were married, the question would have been met with an incredulous stare and a "What? Was Jesus married?" The vast majority would have given a short negative reply, perhaps prefixing it with a "What a silly question" or some similar expression. In Christian churches throughout the world the question would have been readily answered with a "No" — if it were asked there at all.

Since the popular fiction novel, *The Da Vinci Code* by Dan Brown was published in 2003 — and apparently over 80 million copies were sold — interest in Jesus' marital status has increased. Dan Brown's fictitious claim that Jesus was married to Mary Magdalene has created a popular issue which many biblical scholars, commentators, church interest groups and lay people are scurrying to address. One hears of many answers other than a simple yes or no:

- A pointless question, for Jesus did not exist.
- Don't know and don't care.
- He may have been, but then again maybe not.

## Chapter 22  Cana

- It's not stated in the Bible that he was, which probably means that he wasn't.
- The Bible is silent of this issue which does not rule out the possibility that he was.
- Whether he was or wasn't is immaterial for it would have no bearing on our salvation.

and so on...

Using the Bible purely as an historical document, one discovers that nowhere is there a statement of whether Jesus was married or not. The absence of a statement that he was not married cannot be taken as an indication that he was. Nor can the absence of a statement that he was married be taken as an indication that he was not married. Suggestions pointing one way or the other can be argued but the onus of proof would be on those who claim that he was married.

It was a relaxing time for the travellers after the wedding ceremony. Except for a few keen shoppers who were still deciding what to buy for this or that person, the remainder were sitting around in groups involved in idle conversation. The topics jumped around depending on the various interests. The quality of wine on offer was on some lips. The sparkling, enticing display of items for sale held the attention of others. Tour group Gordon was patiently listening to the problems some were having with the local money dispensing machines. A group sitting around a table with Pastor Paul seemed to be involved in more serious discussions. It appeared that John's Marriage in Cana story still held their attention.

Colin had all the others looking at him as he was making a point. 'But Pastor Paul, you have to take into consideration that it was John who wrote this.'

'Yes,' replied the Pastor, 'the event is recorded in St John's Gospel and that's the only place we find it.'

'That's my point. The others don't mention it and I wonder if John really wants us to take the story literally.'

'But Colin,' interrupted Margaret, 'Don't you believe what John has written?'

Her friend Avril came into the discussion and backed her up. 'We were taught that everything written in the Bible is true and that we should believe it whether we understand it or not. I remember our Sunday School teacher, Susan Pfeiffer, telling us that...'

'I think you mean Susan Peters, don't you Avril?' noted Margaret.

'That's right. Peters, not Pfeiffer. She drilled that into us. This is God's word and we must believe it.'

'It's not a matter of believing or not believing,' answered Colin. 'It's a matter of how we understand the story.'

'What do you mean by that Colin?' asked Tony who had been sitting quietly enjoying the wine.

'I think the Evangelist John was wanting us to look past the literal meaning of a lot of what he was writing. There was a deeper purpose to his writing. Why, he even had a dig at those who want to take his writing too seriously and literally.'

'Taking a dig at people?' interrupted Margaret. 'How on earth can you say that, Colin?'

'I'll give you a good example. You remember the story about Nicodemus?'

Margaret, Avril and the others around the table nodded a 'yes'.

'Well, do you remember what Nicodemus said when Jesus told him he had to be born again?'

'Yes,' replied Margaret. 'He said something like an old person can't go back into the womb and be born again. Something like that, wasn't it, Pastor?' And the Pastor nodded his agreement.

'Well, don't you see,' continued Colin, 'John is showing us how silly it is to take some things too literally.'

'And what has that got to do with the story of Jesus turning water into wine?' Avril wanted to know. "There's nothing about being born again in there, is there, Pastor?'

'No, you are right, Avril,' replied Colin before the Pastor could nod his head in agreement. 'He doesn't tell us outright that we should look for a deeper meaning to this story, but there are a lot of small indications. I see the story more as a parable than the report of an actual event.'

A few other people had moved up to this table and were standing around listening. At Colin's last remark several of them all tried to speak at once disagreeing with his views. Pastor Paul saw that a heated argument was likely to break out and he asked for quiet. 'Friends, please! Please! I think we are getting into an area which can't really be discussed here where we have been enjoying this... how can I put it...? This wedding reception. It would probably be a good idea if...'

Here he was interrupted by someone, obviously upset, who called out, 'But this is unbelief, isn't it? Our church doesn't think like this and I'm sure you don't, do you, Pastor?'

'Colin has expressed an interpretation that many accept, and we must not judge it harshly. No, our church does not treat it like this and I naturally follow the church's stand. And I'm sure Colin would have a lot of very thoughtful things to say about this event, but in different circumstances. Are you all with me on that?'

There was a general nodding of agreement and the topic was changed. Then someone asked Tony, 'Where's your mate? He's usually in on these discussions.'

'Who? Andrew?' Tony replied. 'I've no idea. Isn't he here somewhere, probably eating more cake or sampling some more wine.'

Another voice offered the answer. 'I saw him and Sarah making their way back towards the Wedding Church.'

'Maybe they were going back to get married too,' someone else commented. This was met with laughter and some light-hearted, albeit suggestive, remarks. Most had moved on from how to interpret the story of Jesus changing water into wine and got back to enjoying their trip rather than arguing theology.

## Chapter 23

# Into the West

The tour continued and was now headed towards the west; towards the Mediterranean Sea where, if the four Gospels have accounted for all of Jesus' wanderings, his footprints would not be found. Apart from a few trips up to Jerusalem for the major Jewish festivals, he spent most of his time teaching and preaching in his homeland of Galilee. The focus here in the west would not be on Jesus' life and activities but religious themes would still appear, for as Sarah told her listeners several times throughout the tour, there are few places in her country where religion has not left some sort of a mark.

Directly west of the Sea of Galilee is a land projection into the Mediterranean which interrupts an otherwise even sweep of coastline. This is where the mountain chain of Mt Carmel is resisting erosion and appears to be making a defiant statement to the persistent beating of the waves against its base.

Mt Carmel is a long mountain range, about forty kilometres long (yes, really forty!), which runs in a S-E to N-W direction ending in fairly steep slopes which lead down to the Mediterranean coast. At this point is the city of Haifa. From the summit of this N-W point which is about 500 metres high, there is a fine view of this port city and the blue waters of the Mediterranean fading into the west. At times Mt Carmel can refer to this headland rather than the whole length of the range

The range forms a barrier for traffic moving from the south of Israel to the north and in the past has often figured in army movements. Because of the strategic placing of this range of mountains the area has witnessed several significant battles in Israel's history.

Mt Carmel was also the setting for one of those great Old Testament stories, itself a sort of a battle. This one was a competition between Baal, championed by 450 prophets, and the Lord of Israel, worshipped by the prophet Elijah. The duel was to see which god would/could send down fire to burn a bull sacrifice each side had prepared. This rather blood-thirsty story is recorded in 1 Kings 18: 16-46.

The group was relaxing in a park in Haifa after having viewed the spectacular Shrine of the Bab from the top of Mt Carmel.

'Margaret, do you ever think about that story of Elijah and the Prophets of Baal?' It was Tony who asked the question. Others looked up, wondering what he was getting at this time.

'What do you mean; do I ever think about it?'

'You know, if for some reason it comes up. Probably not so often in everyday conversation, but at church, Bible study perhaps.'

'Well,' replied Margaret, 'I remember learning the story at Sunday School, and I suppose it has come up from time to time but I can't really remember when. So why the question? Knowing you, there must be some reason for it.'

'I was really thinking about those 450 prophets of Baal,' explained Tony.

'What about them? They didn't believe in the true God, so they were killed.'

'I wonder did they put up a fight, or did they just lie down and allow themselves to be slaughtered. Pretty messy, I would think.'

'The things you come up with!' said Avril. 'The Bible says that's what happened, and we don't really have to think about it. How this might have happened, or how that might have happened. If God wanted us to know those things he would have had it in the Bible for us to read.'

Tony seemed to ignore Avril's comment and continued, 'I read that there is this monument up on Mt Carmel somewhere, but we didn't visit it. It shows Elijah with a sword held high above his head stamping on the head of one of the defeated prophets of Baal. A thought crossed my mind when I saw that photo; I wonder if that is what we should do to those who have a different religion from ours?'

Colin entered the conversation before Margaret or Avril could respond to Tony. He could see that they were a little taken aback and didn't really know what to say. 'I would hope that this barbaric attitude to adherents of faiths other than one's own would best be left in the distant past.'

'But you can't get away from the fact that Elijah was right and the others were wrong,' Margaret had thought of something to say and interrupted Colin.

He continued however, 'Even if we believe we are right we shouldn't have a feeling of superiority over those who don't think like we do. If we think they are wrong, we certainly should not take extreme action against them.'

Andrew then felt that he had to express his thoughts.

'Wait a minute,' he began, 'in this whole area of faith, religion and beliefs we should not think in terms of right or wrong. I have my beliefs, my faith, which works for me. It's right for me, if you want to put it like that. I can be enthusiastic and speak positively about what I believe. However, in doing this I should guard against being negative towards what others might believe; avoid saying that their faith is wrong.'

Both Margaret and Avril as well as a few others were shaking their heads.

'That's not how we were brought up,' someone was heard to say.

'No listen. It's this idea that mine is the only true religion and that everyone else is wrong is what causes so much strife in the world — always has, does today, and always will!' Andrew was more passionate than he had been on the whole trip. People were surprised that he regarded religious beliefs so fervently.

During this discussion people had, from time to time, looked towards Pastor Paul wondering what he might say. He had said nothing. He now entered the conversation.

'If I can make an observation?' he began by asking the hypothetical question. 'I think it's ironic that we should be having a discussion like this just after visiting the Shrine of the Bab.'

'The Shrine of the Bab? I don't see the connection,' someone said.

'No, I'm a little disappointed that we didn't take time to talk about the Bab and the Baha'i faith. All we did was go up the mountain to look down on the shrine and the gardens.'

'But this is a Christian pilgrimage, after all,' said Colin.

'Yes, I understand that,' conceded Pastor Paul, 'but it does seem a little narrow-minded not to try to get some understanding of what they believe.'

'So how is all of this related to Elijah?' Margaret wanted to know.

'It's not so much related to Elijah, but rather as one answer to our discussion of religious tolerance. I'm no expert on the Bab or the Baha'i faith. I've just learnt a bit from a neighbour of mine. He explained it to me by saying that there is one God but many messengers.'

'OK. But what does that really mean?'

'As I understand it,' Pastor Paul continued, 'there is one God who is the source of creation. All the great religions of the world pay respect to him in their own way. Let's face it, we cannot understand, or know God, and so each group has come up with

## Chapter 23  Into the West

its own interpretation. Each of these religions in its own way is a messenger bringing us an understanding of the one God.'

Colin was nodding. 'So, the Baha'i people like to think that there is a basic unity within the various religions, each directing their thoughts towards the same God. And each one adding a bit more to our understanding of the Divine. If that is the case each should respect the other and not abuse one another. I see what you are getting at, Pastor.'

'Something like that, yes, Colin. And similarly, they see, as we Christians do also, that all people are created equal and should be respected and treated with love and dignity.'

'Yes,' came in Tony, 'even though we do not agree with them. Certainly not slaughter them!'

Pastor Paul cut him off. 'I think we should leave the discussion at that, Tony. But it's interesting, isn't it? It does not matter what we are visiting here in Israel, you people always come up with different ideas. I wonder what you will have to say in Caesarea Maritima which we will be visiting after lunch? No, wait a minute. We will be having lunch there, if I'm not mistaken.'

Caesarea Maritima today is predominantly an archaeological site where attempts are being made to bring back to life some of the glory which was once part of a thriving, bustling capital city. This city grew when the power and wealth of Herod the Great took an old Phoenician naval base to the south of Mt Carmel, and made it into a large port and royal city. He built breakwaters into the temperamental Mediterranean Sea making a safe haven for ships. He built a palace and around it a city of over 100 000 inhabitants. He named his new creation Caesarea in honour of Augustus Caesar, the Roman emperor at the time.

The site he chose lacked fresh water and so he had an aqueduct constructed, which brought water from Mt Carmel sixteen kilometres to the north. This is the first ancient evidence to be seen when visitors approach the old city site. It runs along the sandy beaches of the Mediterranean. What a surprise. Two thousand years ago it had been built and it is still standing proudly. Storm and tsunamis, earth tremors and the ravages of time have not wrought much change to the solid workmanship.

But what of the city? 'What city?' one could well ask as our tour group made its way towards the eating places which had grown up here. 'A pie, a pie!' A cry was heard from beneath the fluttering boxing kangaroo. 'My smart phone for a pie!' Oh, what travelling for fourteen days in the land of the falafel can do to one. An overdue lunch can do strange things as well.

But how could 2000 years have done so much damage to a solidly constructed city? Why should it be that after this time the foundations of Herod's achievement needed to be dug up from metres below the present land surface, or that the mighty rock walls of the port lie deep beneath the water? Has time created so much change? Clearly it has. Time has seen the ebb and flow of countries vying for supremacy in the Levant. Caesarea has suffered in that struggle.

In Herod's time it was great; one of his finest building achievements, and he had many! As a friend of Rome in the Roman world he had no challengers. After his death — and he was not granted many years to enjoy his seaside paradise — the Roman governors lived here. For them this was preferable to living in Jerusalem, the Jewish capital of the area. They would pop up there when needed.

Pontius Pilate lived here in Herod's palace when Jesus walked the pathways of Galilee. Here in Caesarea, back in 1961, a dedicatory stone to the Emperor Tiberius with the inscription "Pontius Pilate, prefect of Judea" was located. A replica of this stone can be still seen on the site of the previous palace. The Roman governors did add to its beauty for it was they who lived there and so would enjoy the benefits. The end of Roman rule in the region, however, signalled the beginning of the end for this city.

The ebbing and flowing of powers was about to begin and the beauty of the city suffered, ending in destruction. It saw occupation by Romans, Arabs, Crusaders, Saladin (Arabs again), Crusaders again, and finally Mamluks who completely raised the city. The ruins lay there, sinking into the waters of the Mediterranean, buried by the sands of time until the 1950s when excavations began uncovering its long history.

Today the process of piecing back its royal buildings and playgrounds is not easy. Fields of ancient building materials bear witness to this. Rebuilding moves slowly.

Time however, for a tour group enjoying each other's company, challenged by the sites and what they represent, does not. It moves quickly. This night, after trowelling through the debris of time, the high-rise Tel Aviv hotel would usher in their penultimate day in Israel. An undisturbed sleep would ensure that the sites of this last touring day would be appreciated and enjoyed.

*Ancient aqueduct which previously took water to the city of Caesarea Maritima.*

# Chapter 24

# Jaffa

JERUSALEM, IN THE TEMPLE FORECOURT, CIRCA 400 BCE:

Gather 'round Folk. I want to tell you about this chap called Jonah, and what he thought about a city called Nineveh and its people.

Jonah was a simple country lad who spent most of his time out in the hills with his dad's flock of sheep and goats. His days were long and boring, so he had a lot of time to sit and think, to ponder the evil in the world, to daydream, and to long for better times. He would often spend time talking to special members of his flock. They would look up, attentive but oft times not, and say nothing. It was also mentioned around the district that he talked to rocks and ridges. These also remained unmoved.

One singularly hot afternoon when he was sitting gazing at a cleft in a cliff face, imagining cool water flowing from it, he heard his name being called.

'Jonah!'

He looked around but saw no one. The flock stared blankly into space.

'Jonah!' It seemed to be coming from the dry, brown cliff face. 'Jonah, go home and tell your dad to find someone else to mind his animals. I have a more important job for you.'

'What is this? Who is speaking? What's going on here?'

'I am the Lord, Jonah. The God of your ancestors, your dad's God and your God too. I want you to go over to Nineveh. Their wickedness has got out of hand and I want you to preach to them. Make them see the error of their ways.'

'Go to Nineveh? That god-forsaken place? You can't be serious, Lord!'

'God-forsaken, maybe. But that's not how I want it to be. And I want you to help me do something about it.'

Jonah argued, but the Lord insisted, and to save further argument — it was a hot, tiring day — Jonah agreed. But a plan B was taking shape in his mind. 'I'll pack my bag,' he thought, 'and head off. The Lord will think that I'm on my way to Nineveh over there in the east, but I'll hitch-hike down to Joppa and catch a boat heading west, perhaps to Tarshish. I've heard a lot about Tarshish and wouldn't mind seeing the bright lights there. The Lord will be waiting for me over near Nineveh and won't know where I've gotten to.'

And this is what he did. He got down to Joppa. He had enough in his pocket to pay for a single berth on a Tarshish-bound boat and he was soon on board. As the sailors got the vessel fully loaded and under way, Jonah sat on the deck thinking, 'This is the life. Sorry God, to have pulled a swiftie on you.'

The trouble was that Jonah must have forgotten the words of a psalm which he surely would have heard in the local synagogue. You know the one I mean? I'll remind you:

*Where can I go from your Spirit?*
*Where can I flee from your presence?*
*If I go up to the heavens, you are there.*
*If I make my bed in the depths, you are there.*

And so it goes on, leaving no doubt that the Lord is everywhere and it would not be easy to flee from him.

The ship was soon underway and up on the top deck the breeze had stiffened enough for Jonah to feel uncomfortable. He decided to go down to his cabin. As he went he noticed dark clouds mounting in the west. 'We're in for some nasty weather,' he thought to himself.

Yes, the Lord had sent a storm. It swept towards the ship and

## Chapter 24  Jaffa

met it head on. It grew in intensity. The wind screamed. The waters raged. The ship reared. The crew struggled. How much of this storm could their old ship stand? Anymore and it would surely start to break in pieces. The captain cursed and the crew cried out to their gods.

But the storm came on and the order was given to lessen their load and start throwing the cargo into the sea. And Jonah? During all this commotion he was below, fast asleep in his cabin.

Then the blame game began. Who caused this monster storm to appear? It didn't take long for fingers to be pointed at Jonah, for he had unwisely let slip that he had outsmarted his god who thought he was headed for Nineveh. Apparently, his god was not so easily conned. He was dragged up on deck. The present circumstances forced Jonah to come to his senses. He was ready to take the blame and suggested that the crew throw him overboard. In this way his god might be appeased and show sympathy to the heathen crew and save their boat.

The sailors were mostly decent blokes and didn't take Jonah up on his suggestion although some did agree with his solution. They decided to try and row back to Joppa now that the ship was lighter. They tried but to no avail. The wind grew even stronger and the sea rougher. Finally, completely exhausted and dreading the thought of their own drowning, they abandoned oars, took Jonah and tossed him overboard; but not before asking the Lord to forgive them for what they were about to do. The Lord clearly had compassion on these reluctant assassins for the wind stopped and the sea calmed.

And Jonah? As luck would have it, the Lord had arranged for a large fish to be in the vicinity. It was waiting for this moment and when it saw Jonah making his clumsy entry into the water, it glided up and swallowed him, thus saving the failed missionary from a watery grave. Jonah ended up staying three days and three nights in the belly of that marine monster.

He could never get comfortable during his stay there. After all, he was a country boy, used to open spaces, the wide blue sky and fresh air. In this stomach apartment it was cramped, moist and gloomy. The only light was the faint glow which came from several florescent worms which had been surprised and swallowed. And how he missed the smell of his goats. He also suffered from claustrophobia and his situation was becoming unbearable. Then, from the confines of his gastric cell, he called to the Lord, admitting his stupidity and promising to do better in the future.

And the Lord heard Jonah in his despair and told the fish to spew him out onto dry land. Now there he lay ashore on a pebbly beach. He awoke to the voices of noisy children who were holding their noses and making rude comments about him. He realised himself that he was overdue for a bath and so he ignored them and headed back to his home. He had not gone very far when the word of the Lord came to him again.

'Oh, no,' he sighed, anticipating what the Lord was about to say to him. This time however he replied with a "yes" that meant *yes* and not a "yes" that meant *no*. 'And,' he directed back to the Lord, 'tell me what to say for I am not used to talking to people.'

So, Jonah headed east and eventually arrived at the great city of Nineveh; no small oasis with date palms and a few mud huts. No, it would take a good three days to make one's way through its bustling streets. Jonah got straight to work, shouting out the message that the Lord had put on his lips.

And the result was absolutely startling. The people listened. Everyone listened, from the beggars to the king. The king indeed was so moved that he removed his royal robes, put a hessian bag around his shoulders and sat down in the dirt and ashes. From this unlikely position he issued a royal decree commanding all his subjects and their animals to start fasting, put on sackcloth, give up their evil ways and repent before Jonah's god.

## Chapter 24  Jaffa

The subjects did as they were told. They probably knew from past experience what would happen to any who chose to disobey the king. Soon the whole city was decked out in all manner of hessian bags, people and animals alike. This pleased the Lord and he showed compassion on them all. He didn't destroy them and their city as he had planned.

And they all lived happily ever after? No! That's not the end of this story. Jonah wasn't at all happy with what had happened. He just could not tolerate his Lord loving these heathen people. He maintained that the Lord should keep his love for his chosen people, and for them alone. He sulked. He went into a decline, threatening to take his own life. He sat down outside the city and brooded in the scorching sun.

In spite of this attitude, the Lord had not forgotten him and caused a shade tree to grow over him to provide some protection. This really pleased Jonah and he began meaningful conversations with the tree. But the tree didn't really listen to him. This did not stop Jonah growing to love the tree.

But alas! God then caused a worm to come and chew the tree down to its roots, which left Jonah exposed to the weather once again. To make matters worse, God sent a heat wave with scorching winds.

Jonah had had enough. Life was no longer worth living. Why was this happening to him? Why had God killed the tree that he loved? Where to now?

God had the last word. 'I don't understand you, Jonah,' he said. 'You are so upset about the tree. But you had nothing to do with its existence. And it is only a tree. How can you not be concerned about all those thousands of people in Nineveh? Oh! And their flocks as well?'

The wheels kept rolling. The coach was making its way towards the old port of Jaffa, which today is part of the modern city of Tel Aviv. Tony had been quiet, taking in the landscape as it moved past. With his eyes still outside he addressed Andrew, 'You haven't seen any orange orchards, have you? I've kept my eyes peeled for the last half hour and have not seen any.'

Andrew was somewhat surprised by the question which seemed completely unrelated to their present situation.

'No,' he replied, 'and I haven't seen any kangaroos either, nor coal mines. Why on earth are you looking for orchards of oranges?'

'We are coming into Jaffa. Haven't you ever heard of Jaffa oranges? My Mum was always talking about them.'

'Navel and Valencia, yes; but Jaffa? No, I've never heard of them.' Andrew was happy enough to talk about oranges, for there was no tour topic worrying him at that moment. 'Oh, that's right, I've also heard of blood oranges. Have you ever heard of blood oranges?'

'Yes, I've eaten blood oranges,' replied Tony. 'There were some which were completely red inside and other with just streaks of red in their flesh.'

'They're the ones,' continued Andrew, 'and I remember cutting a blood orange into pieces some years ago just when my sister happened to come into the room. "Oh, shit!" I cried out "I've cut my finger and there's blood everywhere." Then I quickly wrapped a handkerchief around my finger. Julie was really worried and wanted to get the band-aids. "Don't worry," I said, "it will be OK, but we can't waste the orange." I then picked up a piece which was all bloody-looking and started sucking it. "Gross!" was all she could say.'

'Didn't she know about blood oranges?' Tony asked an obvious question.

'She didn't then but she does now,' laughed Andrew. He then

## Chapter 24  Jaffa

directed his voice to Sarah who was sitting at the front of the bus. 'Hey Sarah, do you know anything about Jaffa oranges?'

Sarah turned the microphone on. 'We are coming into the old town of Jaffa and someone has asked me about Jaffa oranges. Maybe others of you have heard about them too. I'm no expert on their history, but I do know that they used to produce a lot of oranges around here. They were exported all over Europe. Now, as you have probably noticed, there are no orchards to be seen. What? No, that's true. Maybe you weren't even looking for orange orchards as Colin back there suggested. I know you can still buy Jaffa oranges here in Israel, but they probably come from Spain or Portugal.'

She stopped talking for a short while and then continued, 'Getting back to the old port of Jaffa; it's now part of the modern city of Tel Aviv, but it has retained some of its old buildings and charm. Some of you may have seen murals of a large fish, or perhaps a whale, on some walls. Now if you look to the right you will see a sculpture of a big fish. What's that Pastor Paul?'

Pastor Paul then spoke loudly from the centre of the bus, 'The Jaffa of today was the Joppa of Biblical times. That's where Jonah went to catch a boat to run away from the Lord.'

'That's right, but we will hear more about that later on. Yes, you will have time later to come back to that large fish sculpture if you want to. You can crawl all over it if that's what you'd like to do, but be careful that you don't slip into the water. I've been told it's quite slippery. If you do fall in don't worry, for it will not swallow you.'

'So where to now, Sarah?' someone wanted to know amid the laughter.

'We will be stopping in the old town just up the hill here. First, we will walk down an old street to a house called Simon the Tanner's House. We won't be able to go inside for there are people living there. The relevance of this, I've been told many times, relates back to a lesser-known episode in the New Testament. It is about the Apostle Peter having a vision while he was up on top of the roof praying.'

'So, are you going to tell us the whole story?'

'No. Perhaps you can catch Pastor Paul later. Or shall I set you some homework for tonight? I can say however that it has some similar ideas to the Jonah story.'

'Did Peter dream of going fishing and catching a big fish?' someone wanted to know.

'No, but it's something you can think about. So now we will have a quick look at this old house and others around it. I have nothing more to say about it, so you can make your own way there and be back in, say 30 minutes.'

'Where are we going to meet?'

'Oh, yes, I forgot. We will meet under that tree there where there are seats for most of us. Then Tony will refresh us about Jonah and his adventures.'

'What! Is he going to read the whole Book of Jonah? How many chapters is that?'

'No, don't worry, Colin. He will tell us in his own words.'

Not everyone went off to visit the old house of Simon the Tanner. Most did but the others remained sitting under the tree waiting. It was not long before everyone had returned, and Tony could begin relating his version of Jonah and the Whale. Margaret had moved over to be next to Pastor Paul by the time Tony had finished telling the well-known (perhaps not) story. Her stern face and fixed jaw clearly indicated that she had several issues she wished to discuss. This could only be about Tony's presentation.

'Pastor Paul, he's taken it a bit far this time, hasn't he? He shouldn't be telling stories from God's Word like that, should he?'

'He does have a turn of phrase, doesn't he?' replied the

minister. 'I certainly wouldn't — couldn't either — relate the Jonah story like that. But as far as I can remember, he has all of his facts correct.'

'But he made a mockery of the whole thing,' insisted Margaret. 'He gave the impression that the whale didn't really swallow Jonah; that the whole story was just an ancient fairytale.'

'Perhaps, not a fairytale, Margaret, but you will find that most Bible scholars today do see this story as an allegory or a parable. It is important to see the main message in the story rather than just the story for itself.'

'I don't know! What's Christianity coming to if we are told not to believe the Bible anymore?'

Pastor Paul was saved from further discussion on Jonah, or Bible interpretation generally, by Sarah who interrupted and told everyone that the bus would be arriving back in thirty minutes and if anyone wanted to go back and see the sculptured big fish or look through the Church of St Peter they should move off immediately.

That said, she moved over to where Andrew and Tony were now seated. Tony stood up when she arrived and excused himself. 'I'm going back to have a good look at that big fish. There are a few people here I would like to dodge for the moment.'

Sarah caught him before he left. 'Just a minute. I won't swallow you! I want to thank you very much for telling the Jonah story. You really had the people in, although as we now know for sure, some looked a little worried about how you put some things.'

'My pleasure, Sarah. And don't worry. They'll soon all get over it. I'll leave you two.'

Once Tony had gone, Sarah turned to Andrew. 'And how did you find that?'

'Just as I would have expected. I could have told you he would upset some people. But there's no great damage done.'

'But what about things generally. Are you feeling well and enjoying yourself?'

'I can't really complain. Everyone has been going out of their way to help me. A bit much on some occasions.'

'I'm pleased about that. I would have liked to help you more, but something always seems to get in the way. I'm sorry about that.'

'That's OK. I understand. But tell me, do you have anything you need to do just at this moment?'

'No, I'll just wait around for the bus to arrive,' Sarah replied.

Andrew was silent for a moment and then he said, 'Would you like to come with me and we could have a cup of coffee together at that place I saw up the road?'

'Oh!' and Sarah blushed. 'It's not a good idea for tour guides to fraternise too much with handsome young members of the group.'

Sarah was so excited that Andrew had asked her. She had often quietly looked in his direction thinking how she would like to get to know him a little better. He appeared so quiet and almost shy. But this was probably exaggerated in the presence of Tony who was so outgoing. Sure, Tony would be fun to be with, but Andrew seemed to have something much deeper and this intrigued her. She hoped her response, said really as a joke, would not offend him.

Andrew did seem disappointed with her reply. 'But it's only a cup of coffee, and I promise to be on my best behaviour.'

'I can't imagine you being on anything but your best behaviour,' smiled Sarah. 'And why not? I would very much enjoy having a cup of coffee with you without everyone else around.'

They moved off together and Andrew felt a little uncomfortable when Sarah put her arm through his as though it were the natural thing to do. But he enjoyed the feeling of being so close to her.

The coffee was tasting particularly good.

'It's hard to realise that there's only a couple of days to go before my tour is over,' Andrew appeared to be a little sad with the thought.

'Yes, I know. It only seems like yesterday that I met you all there at the Jordanian border.'

'And looking back,' continued Andrew, 'everything has gone so quickly. We've seen so much and so much has changed for me. I feel better, that is true, but it's more than that. And Sarah...' Andrew stopped, hesitated but finally continued as she looked intently at him, 'I believe that during that time I have come to know you very well, but I've never managed to tell you how I feel about you.'

Sarah smiled. It was a sincere, understanding smile. Then she said light-heartedly, 'I think we have Tony to blame for that. It was the same with me. Every time I wanted to express how I felt about you he would pop up on the scene.'

Then Andrew laughed. 'That was uncanny. He came along to look after me, and I have appreciated that, but I didn't think he would want to dictate my love life.'

'Love life?' exclaimed Sarah.

'You know what I mean; my personal life.'

'Oh! I thought for a while that you...'

Andrew interrupted her, not wanting those emotions to reappear that have always held him spellbound and made him dumb. He stammered out, 'Love. Yes, that's the word. I love you, Sarah. There is no other word for it.'

'Oh, Andrew,' breathed Sarah as she reached over and clasp his hand in hers, avoiding knocking over a cup of coffee by the barest of margins.

Andrew continued, 'I have been wanting to spend more time with you but with you having all your responsibilities I know it was not possible.'

'I understand, Andrew,' said Sarah. 'I also have wanted that, but people notice things and believe me, they don't take kindly to any leaders neglecting their job and showing favouritism.'

'I have the feeling that quite a few of the group know how I feel about you. What do you think?'

'That's probably true,' agreed Sarah. 'Gordon has had a word to me, but he is not worried. He said he was pleased with the way we have handled the situation.'

'The question is what now, Sarah?' asked Andrew. 'We finally are sure of our feelings for each other. Have we any idea of what next? Will our friendship just peter out in a few days when I have to fly back to Australia?'

'I hope not, Andrew. I want it to continue. And it has really just started. I have an idea. Tomorrow you have the afternoon free; well, not actually free but time to visit the Carmel markets in Tel Aviv. You probably don't know but I live in Tel Aviv when I am not travelling with a tour group. I have a unit there. I'm sure no one would notice if we missed the markets. They are so big and crowded anyway. We could spend some time in my unit without anyone interrupting us; Tony for instance.'

'Oh, I do hope we can arrange that. It will give us time to look at things rationally,' said Andrew.

'I hope not too rationally,' laughed Sarah. She was looking down the street and suddenly laughed louder. 'Do you see who is coming towards us?'

Andrew turned around in his chair and shook his head. 'Who would believe it! But you are too late this time Tony!'

\* \* \*

## Chapter 24  Jaffa

### Extract from Andrew's travel diary:

It's all over now bar the shouting. Shouting? Probably crying! No doubt it will be for some people. I don't want it to be over, but what is the alternative? I could become very morbid and that would hardly cheer me up. Why not write about something more trite which will keep my mind off the trip back home?

A good friend of my mother, Carol (and I know her very well too), who travels quite extensively, comes home and colourfully relates her overseas experiences to us punctuated with terms such as "our limo driver", "champers", "the Qantas Lounge", "five stars", "twenty-four-hour room service". You get the trend? And the Portuguese wine regions she visited, the Eiffel Tower or the Guggenheim in New York — to name but a few — don't really sound like the places I would go very far out of my way to visit for they are near the bottom of my bucket. But we each have our own interests and needs and bring home different memories!

To be fair, she is not only interested in her own travels but also expresses interest in other people's trips. I remember when my dad arrived home from a trip to China one of the first questions she asked was, "How was the accommodation?"

"Carol, my dear," I can remember my dad saying, "my single supplement gave me no less than a queen-sized bed nightly, and indeed in one hotel, two queen-sized beds in the one room. I felt like a king surrounded by all those queens. I slept in a different spot on each of the four nights I was there!" He was probably only kidding; but then again, knowing my father.

I think it will be wise to jot down some accommodation notes in anticipation of her questions when I arrive back home.

<u>Jerusalem:</u>
Our Jerusalem hotel merged beautifully into the hillside. Here

fate gave me a third-floor room. This proved to be a problem in itself for I was always confused whether to go up or down to get to my home base there. It was a problem wherever I was in the hotel. Who ever heard of checking in at the front desk and then having to go DOWN to get to the third floor? And I could never remember whether to take lifts A, which took me to one section of the huge hotel or lifts B, which had me trying to open the wrong door. I could dream of that ideal(?) situation where trying to open the wrong door might lead to all manner of relationships. "Oh, hello," said the young lady who was clearly about to go to bed. "Can I help you?" But I won't go further with that. Even Carol would probably doubt me.

Tiberius:

Tiberius found me in a room on the second floor (i.e. the floor above the main reception area, unlike that in Jerusalem), and I always walked up one flight of stairs to get there. The room overlooked the Sea of Galilee. How wonderful a place to pull the curtains and say, "Good morning" or "Good night" to the world outside. And here I could spend time sitting on the balcony daydreaming, meditating, projecting myself back two millennia. This is peace. This is contentment. Embrace me with your quietude, oh sweet waters!

Back to Mum's friend Carol. "But how many stars?" she would want to know.

You know, Carol, there on my balcony overlooking the Sea of Galilee, with the clear sky above, I thought of Abraham (of Biblical fame, remember?) when the Lord took him outside and said, "Look up at the heavens and count the stars — if indeed you can count them." I never yet have looked in a Michelin star chart to see if I've had a good night's sleep.

## Chapter 24  Jaffa

<u>Tel Aviv:</u>

In Tel Aviv I have reached great heights — floor eight. Marvellous, I think, I can watch the sun setting over the Mediterranean. Bad thinking!! Some rather unimaginative architect had drawn the plans with my room looking east, away from the gentle sea breezes, away from the cooling waters of the Mediterranean. And what do I see as a substitute? I see the tops of emerging sky-scrapers in the distance, the tops of tenement blocks and the dust and noise of a building site in the foreground. That's the luck of the draw, I suppose.

As King David of old, my eye ran over the flat rooftops, but apparently this was not the time for bathing. Tony was especially disappointed! Even if it had been that evocative hour, the rooftops in my view allowed no room for rooftop bathing.

Oh dear! They seemed to be the depositories for unused, worn out and broken household stuff. I can imagine the householder below these flat-topped roofs thinking, "out of sight (up there on the roof), out of mind." No, mate. Not out of sight of the visitor who pulls the hotel room curtain aside to see the blue Mediterranean. And I thought of my Mum who is always agonising about my Dad's stores of treasures which may be of use some day. "Thank God we don't have flat rooftops," would be her immediate response to this Tel Aviv scene.

Were Carol to be given a room such as mine here she would have been down the eight floors to reception before opening her bags. But this is purely speculative for she would have booked a first-class suite in the first place. These, no doubt, would have a Mediterranean view.

*Now that's a fish! It's stranded in a fountain in Jaffa.*

# Chapter 25

# Sarona

"We visit Sarona the home of the Templars." This was a short item listed near the end of a crowded itinerary which had briefly outlined the tour of Israel. Bethlehem, The Stations of the Cross, Sea of Galilee, Cana; names like this rang a loud Christian bell for members of this pilgrim group. Whereas the bell did ring more loudly for some than for others, it could be heard, albeit sometimes faintly.

But Sarona? Templars? Who, or what, or where, or why is this?

At breakfast on the morning of this scheduled visit, Frances Gersekowski had confronted Gordon, the tour leader. 'Gordon, there is a mistake in your itinerary for today.'

'Oh? What have I done wrong this time, Frances?' replied Gordon, wondering where this was headed. It wasn't the first time Frances had chipped him about something.

'It's about Sarona. I googled it before we came on the trip for I had never heard of it before.'

'Fair enough, but what's the problem?'

'Well you say it is "the home of the Templars". That in itself is a bit funny, but the problem is with the word "Templars". The word should end with "ers" and not "ars". Templars and Templers refer to two completely different groups of people.'

Gordon was looking a little embarrassed realising that if Frances was correct — and she probably was — this typo on the itinerary would be giving the wrong information. He looked at her waiting for some more detail.

Frances began explaining. 'Yes, the Templars, or Knights Templar was a Catholic Military Order of Knights involved in the Crusades in the twelfth and thirteenth centuries. They had nothing to do with Sarona. Here, we are talking about the Templers.'

'Oh dear,' said Gordon, 'if you are right, if you're sure of this, Frances, I shall have to let everyone know of the error. For most, I'm sure it wouldn't worry them if was an "a" or an "e". And I'll make sure it's corrected on my future itineraries. Thank you for pointing this out to me.'

Sarona turned out to be a restful, peaceful piece of Eden in the midst of high-rise Tel Aviv. Green lawns, flowers, shrubs and trees, lily-covered ponds and children's playgrounds separated newly restored European-styled dwellings. The visitors were taken by surprise.

To understand Sarona it is necessary to travel back in time to before the existence of the modern city of Tel Aviv. This site was on the coastal lowlands of Palestine named the Plains of Sharon. A group of German people settled here, and they named their settlement Scharona, after the traditional name of the area. This has now become Sarona.

Why did a group of German citizens leave their European homeland and settle here? The time machine will need to go back 160 years and travel to Württemberg in southern Germany. Here in the mid-nineteenth century a pietism movement within the Lutheran Church put itself offside with the established church. This group was known as the Tempelgesellschaft (Temple Society) which we now know as the Templers.

They looked particularly to 1 Cor.3:16 (*Don't you know that you yourselves are God's temple and that God's spirit lives in you?*) and 1 Peter 2:5 (*You also, like living stones, are being built into a spiritual house to be a holy priesthood, offering spiritual sacrifices acceptable to God — through Jesus Christ.)* for the basics of their approach to Christian living. The godliness which they showed in everyday living was, for them, more important than following organised religious formalities. The rift with the main Lutheran Church became inevitable when the Templers adopted millennial beliefs. A major factor in the group's migrating to Palestine was the thought that their strong spiritual beliefs would promote the rebuilding of the temple on Mount Zion. This in turn would hasten the second coming of Christ.

They were duly excommunicated from the mother church and groups did migrate to Palestine to practise their religious freedom. They purchased land and established agricultural settlements. Sarona was one of these. Years of hard, dedicated work created successful enterprises, which showed the way for other settlements as well.

But the twentieth century brought two world wars and Germany was the loser in both. This had repercussions for German citizens throughout the world and not only in Germany itself. 1919 saw most of the Templers in Palestine expelled by the British and placed in internment camps in Egypt. On returning in 1921 they had to begin rebuilding their deteriorated homes and fields.

Then came World War 2 and again the German citizens in Palestine were interned. In 1941 most of the people living in Sarona (functioning as an internment camp at this time) were shipped to Australia. Here they were placed in an internment camp at Tatura near Shepparton in Victoria. They had to leave their home, land and belongings never to be allowed back.

For years the European-styled houses of the Templers in Sarona gradually deteriorated. However, their significance in the heritage history of Israel has now been recognised. Many of the houses have not been demolished but renovated and their surrounds beautified. The homes with their shuttered windows, small balconies and sloped rooves contrast greatly with the high-rise city beside them.

Now, on their last touring day in Israel, Gordon's chargers, not having distinguished from Sarah's oral introduction whether they would be enjoying "the home of the Templars" or " the home of the Templers", were scattered throughout this extraordinary block in Tel Aviv. They are experiencing an oasis of charm and beauty.

From their seat under a palm tree Phillip and Kaye can watch groups of beautiful people, top-enders, caressing their latte macchiatos and skinny chinos while lamenting the price increase of their next Mercedes or their Calypso holiday. Margaret and Avril stroll past elderly couples sitting beside the lily pond pondering youthful times. The Gersekowskis and the Wallers, themselves enjoying something amber give but a casual glance towards the students frolicking on the lawns. Pastor Paul's and Julie's hands go to their wallets as they see the glitterati checking out the latest additions to the boutiques, but hoping that the few NIDs still there might buy some last-minute mementoes.

This small piece of Israel with its restored residences and replanted gardens and lawns has come a long way from the malaria-infested swamps which claimed the lives of so many of those nineteenth century Templers who chose to practise their religious freedom here. It's green lawns, peaceful ponds and enticing outlets have long forgotten the pain and struggle of the German pioneers. They are magnets for the good life.

'Hey, you two!'

Andrew and Tony, who had been slowly wandering around looking at everything in general, enjoying the last day of their trip, stopped and looked around. They saw Colin brandishing his Canon EOS something-or-other.

'Colin. What's up?'

## Chapter 25  Sarona

'Can I take a photo of you two?'

'With all that gear, I'm sure you could. And we'd be honoured to be imaged by a pro like you!'

'Flattery, flattery. I like it!'

'So where would you like us to stand?' asked Andrew.

'I see just the place,' suggested Tony, pointing to one of the houses-cum-boutiques. 'That one with the signs for BOSS, LACOSTE and Tommy something or another. Two well-dressed gentlemen like us should slot well into that background.'

'Don't know whether well-dressed would describe you correctly.' Colin seemed to have missed Tony's irony. 'But we will go over there. I like these old German-styled houses.'

Colin was still trying to get Tony and Andrew to be sensible when he saw Gordon and Sarah standing, taking in the whole pantomime.

'Sarah, can you talk some sense into these two, and get them to stand still so I can take a photo?' Colin pleaded.

'As if they would listen to me!'

'What's this photo shoot all about, Colin?' Gordon asked.

'I just wanted a photo of the two of them, but they're worse than a couple of puppies.'

'Why here, exactly?' Sarah asked.

'Well,' replied Colin, 'we were looking around for some good background and Tony suggested here.'

'Just as I thought. Just the place to highlight his Target T-shirt.

'And our good looks, don't forget,' added Tony.

'Have fun,' she replied, not taking that conversation any further. 'And don't forget we will be off to the Carmen Markets soon. Plenty of opportunities for good shots there, Colin. Oh, and Andrew, I'll see you there, once we are all off the bus.'

The other three looked at Andrew wondering what that comment was all about.

*Olive tree wood carving from Bethlehem.*

## Chapter 26

# Shalom

Any tour leader will tell you that for an enjoyable, successful tour the welcome and farewell dinners seem to be very close together, belying the days of travelling which separate them. Such was the case for this Holy Land tour.

The little Australian flags placed on dining tables to reserve them for these pilgrims would soon be placed in storage until the next group arrived from down under with their thongs and "How ya goin' Mate?" Tonight however, they were still proudly holding their place, albeit drooped somewhat, for tomorrow Masoud — Driver Most Careful — and his coach would start Gordon and this group on their homeward journey.

At first, he would be making an west/east cross-section through Israel from Tel Aviv on the sea, through the hill country, past Jerusalem and then down past Jericho to the Allenby Crossing on the Jordan River. Here it would be good-bye from him and hello to the Jordanian driver who would continue the journey to Annam, the capital city of Jordan. A short wait, then Emirates Airlines would have the travellers in Dubai in three short hours, the first two shorter than the third. From Dubai those who had been close pilgrim companions would head off to Brisbane, to Perth, Adelaide and then further.

A few sentences make the journey seem short. The reality is much longer and tiring, made worse by the knowledge that the days of enjoyment, of uplifting religious experiences, of close companionship had, too soon so it seemed, come to an end.

However, as everyone was finding out at the farewell dinner each in his or her own way was leaving Israel with more than just an olive wood cross, a red-checked keffiyeh (headscarf) or 20 GB of photos. Many were leaving as changed individuals, changed in a most positive way. People were openly expressing the effect the trip has had on their own faith and their attitude towards others who had different opinions and different interpretations of Holy Scripture.

And regrets? Disappointments? Gordon agreed that it would be most unusual if there were not issues which adversely effected some people. Although present, and fortunately seldom aired openly, these rarely detracted from the positive. They did not during this trip either.

'Let's face it,' said Pastor Paul, 'what sort of dinner conversations would we have had if everyone thought the same way? The only way to learn is to mix with others who have different ideas and attitudes from your own. It makes us think, if we have to justify the way we feel about something.'

It was Margaret Schneider's turn to give a brief account of her experiences. Tony gave Andrew a poke in the ribs. 'I bet she has something to say about us.'

Andrew smiled. 'Well, if she has anything bad to say, you only have yourself to blame. But I'm sure she will not say anything nasty.'

'And yes,' Margaret was saying, 'some of you might think it would not be possible, but my thinking and attitudes have changed — well, a little! Avril and I soon saw that there were a lot of people here who did not think about religion as we do. We were a bit worried thinking how things would work out. But we needn't have worried. I think both Avril and I realise that remembering what we learnt in Sunday School isn't all that there is in being a Christian. And if I can be personal, Tony, and Andrew as well, maybe a few more smacks when you were young would not have hurt; but you have been great companions. I wish you both all the best for what lies ahead.'

Margaret seemed embarrassed, but everyone clapped and cheered, obviously reaffirming her opinion.

Regaining her composure, Margaret continued, 'And, whatever you Tony, or others, might think, Bethlehem is still my favourite site.'

Someone called out, 'Your turn, Tony.'

But Andrew stood up. 'Tony reckons he's said enough during the last two weeks; a lot getting him into trouble. Well almost. I want to say a few things for myself. In football talk, I have pulled up better than I thought I would. Thank you all very much for your consideration and help and your prayers for my recovery. The last two weeks have indeed been a very interesting journey for me. Tony, thank you very much for being here to look after me. But I'm afraid that you might get into trouble from my parents when you get back home to Brisbane. You promised to look after me and get me home safely, but you will be arriving back home without me.'

Andrew stopped. He was struggling to continue. Tony looked at him. Everyone looked at him. Then it struck Tony what Andrew had said.

'Without you? What do you mean?'

'Yes,' said Andrew, 'without me. Heavens this is hard for me to say! As some of you may have noticed, Sarah and I have developed strong feelings for each other. Yes, it's true. Don't give me all the reasons why we are old enough to have more sense, but that's how it is. We had a long talk yesterday and I decided I would stay here in Tel Aviv with Sarah for an extra week. This will give us time to talk things through and decide where to go from there.'

He walked over to Sarah who stood up and embraced him. They kissed.

Gordon stood up but could not make himself heard above the clapping and shouting.

* * *

END

www.ingramcontent.com/pod-product-compliance
Lightning Source LLC
Chambersburg PA
CBHW071340080526
44587CB00017B/2910